CANCER, YOU PICKED THE WRONG GIRL

CANCER, YOU PICKED THE WRONG GIRL

A TRUE STORY

SHORMISTHA MUKHERJEE

HarperCollins *Publishers* India

First published in India by
HarperCollins *Publishers* 2021
A-75, Sector 57, Noida, Uttar Pradesh 201301, India
www.harpercollins.co.in

2 4 6 8 10 9 7 5 3 1

P-ISBN: 978-93-5422-755-4
E-ISBN: 978-93-5422-797-4

Typeset in 11/15.2 Adobe Caslon Pro at
Manipal Technologies Limited, Manipal

Printed and bound at
Thomson Press (India) Ltd

MIX
Paper
FSC® C010615

This book is produced from independently certified FSC® paper
to ensure responsible forest management.

For Anirban.
I have a new idea or a new plan almost every day, and you've never
rolled your eyes. But always encouraged me, every single time.
I hope every person in the world finds a hype man like you.
The world would be a much happier place for sure. I love you.

If the sky that we look upon
Should tumble and fall
Or the mountain should crumble to the sea
I won't cry, I won't cry
No I won't shed a tear
Just as long as you stand, stand by me...

−BEN E. KING, 'STAND BY ME'

You only live once, but if you do it right, once is enough.

−MAE WEST

1

ᗰ

March 11.
It all started with a pedicure.

I kid you not.

I am obsessed with pedicures. Okay, not really the pedicure part of it, which is the soaking and the scraping using prehistoric tools. Really, why has no one bothered to invent pretty-looking pedicure tools? Why do they all look like they'd be perfect at an archaeological dig site?

But let me not digress. The part I love is the massage at the end of it. My eyes start to droop, and sometimes I find myself drooling from the corner of my mouth when the pedicurist presses a thumb into the sole of my foot.

Now, most parlour employees recognize this drooling face and see 'sucker' written all over it. Which is why when I go to pay, they immediately offer me a package. At this point I should whip out a cross, hold it in front of me, and quickly manoeuvre my pedicured feet out of the door. But that never happens. And I end up buying twelve pedicures in one shot. Once, I even bought twenty-five.

It would still end well if I did not end up getting swindled. This is how it goes. I buy a package, and the next time I call to make an appointment, the receptionist sweetly informs me, 'Ma'am, your preferred therapist no longer works with us.' Two problems here. One, I'm not sure why everyone is called a therapist now. Very confusing it makes matters. Especially when you're sitting on a couch talking about your marriage or childhood, and suddenly you are wondering why this therapist is not massaging your feet. Two, I paid for a package of twelve pedicures because of this person's magical ability to make my feet feel like the softest paneer. And now he or she is gone.

And that's exactly what happened to me on that fateful Saturday morning. I had come home from cycling, had a free day ahead of me, and decided to use my package. But when I called the parlour, guess what? Sucker. The therapist had quit.

I put down the phone, most irritated with myself. Lay on the bed. And wondered what to do.

And it struck me, that lump in my breast. The one that was growing. The one I was pushing under my middle-class dhurrie from the annual winter handloom fair.

Maybe I should get it checked.

Let me pause here for a second. To reflect on my stupidity. This lump that I was just about to move my ass on had been around for a while. The thing is, I couldn't remember how long. This was mid-March in 2018, and I'm sure I had felt the lump in December 2017 when I went swimming in Goa. But I had done nothing. Mostly because I was so sure it would be a benign lump or cyst.

That's because I've been getting benign cysts in my lady lumps since I was eighteen.

I remember coming home from college one year and telling my mother about this lump I felt in my breast. And the only reason I would have even noticed it or brought it up is because I had vague memories as a child of my mom talking about being operated for a lump in her breast when she was young.

See, all these disconnected things. How they add up. But I've always been bad at maths, so I guess it just took me too long to work it out.

Anyway, Mom took me to the closest military hospital, or MH, as they are called. My father was in the Air Force at that point in time, so the MH was our go-to for everything. Actually, it's still the go-to for everything, as far as my parents are concerned. But me, I dread them. First of all, they are connected to every unpleasant childhood memory I have. Measles, mumps, tonsils, and warm milk at 6 a.m. Then there's the time I admitted myself into an MH for chickenpox. They put me in a quarantine building that was straight out of the movie *The Shining*. Seriously. I was the only patient in that place. And they gave me a corner room on the first or second floor. A room that was the size of a football field with one solitary metal bed and table.

I was in college, living as a paying guest, and of course my landlady wasn't too thrilled at the thought of having a poxed girl hanging around the house. So, there I was. Alone, sick and hiding under a very rough sheet on a narrow hospital bed in a bare room, where all you could hear was the sound of the leaking tap from the bathroom.

All night the tap leaked, and all night I freaked.

Oh, and the nurse's station was on the ground floor. Which means when the ghosts of that old, dilapidated building chased me down the corridor, their heads spinning back and forth, vomit spewing from their mouth, I would be dead by the time I even reached the stairs. And no one would know.

By morning, I was hungry, sweaty, and crazed. A lot like Jack Nicholson in *The Shining*.

I finally made it out of the hospital that evening. Actually, I escaped. But that's another story.

Getting back to this one.

I remember a thin, long needle being inserted into the lump in my breast. And the results would come in a few days. Was I stressed?

Not in the least bit. At eighteen, breast cancer doesn't even cross your mind.

Well, it most certainly didn't cross mine at forty-four either.

I've always had lumps. I've always been to the gynaecologist. Sometimes, they've examined and dismissed me. Sometimes, they've done a sonography and let me out. No big deal. Apparently, benign lumps are as common as Café Coffee Days.

That's what I was telling myself.

But somewhere, in a dark and scary place in my brain, there was a siren going off. The lump seemed to be growing bigger. It was in the top half of my breast, and now I could easily feel it. Plus, about ten days back, while having a shower, I realized my nipple had gone in. Like, inverted itself totally. I didn't pay much attention, thinking it's okay, maybe this sort of thing happens. It'll pop back out.

But it didn't.

And there I was, lying in bed, staring at the ceiling fan, happily exhausted from having cycled about 30 kilometres that morning. Little did I know the shit was about to hit the fan.

I rolled over, grabbed my phone, and called the gynaecologist. I'd been to her just over a year back for a lump in my breast. I knew the drill. First, I'll have to get an appointment. And preferably in the same year. Really, what is it with doctors being so busy? Do we not have enough of them or are we all just falling sick in hordes? Every time I call this doctor for an appointment, her receptionist will say, 'Hang on.' And then after ten minutes, in a very bored voice, inform me that an appointment is available ten days from now.

Of course I can't wait ten days. Because for over three months I've sat on my ass and watched this lump grow.

Anyway, I called, all prepared to grovel and beg. But luck was on my side. Actually, strike that out. Luck wasn't going to be on my side for a while. The bored lady in her bored voice told me that she'd give me an appointment in three days.

I let out a silent whoop of joy and then proceeded to grovel for a morning appointment. So I could jazz in before work, flash my boobs at the doctor, exchange pleasantries as she dismisses me with a wave, saying, 'It's benign, nothing to worry about.' And then go about my life.

Guess what? I got a morning appointment. Just like that. Easy-peasy.

I lay back on the bed. And I had this strange feeling. This appointment happened too easy. Was the universe trying to tell me something? I tried to shake it off by calling one of my closest friends, Oindrila, or Oinx, as I like to call her. Tucked into a long conversation on just about everything under the sun, I let slip that I had made an appointment with the gynaecologist. She immediately said, 'I'm coming with you.' I was like, 'Why? It's just a stupid lump. I get them all the time. No one needs to come.' But she insisted.

That evening, my husband, Anirban, who was out of town, called. I casually told him that I had an appointment with the gynaecologist, and he said the same thing, 'I'll come.'

Now, in hindsight, I wonder what made the two of them insist on coming. I told both of them that the other one was coming, and this was not a party. And I didn't need a plus-one, or two. But both were strangely insistent.

March 13. The morning of the appointment, I messaged Oinx. Telling her not to come. Telling her that I was PMSing and feeling grumpy, and that I just wanted to be on my own. But she would not take no for an answer. She kept saying, 'You need someone with you.'

So, there we were, the three of us. At the gynaecologist, dressed in our office clothes, talking and texting into our phones, pushing meetings, doing conference calls, sipping coffee. I felt a bit like I had brought the cast of the show *Suits* to the doctor's.

We waited. Because, of course, no appointment can ever happen on time. That would just be blasphemy and totally defeat the reason we're called patients.

And while we waited, I realized we were the lowest in the food chain at the gynaec's. The pregnant people are right on top. They have every visible reason to be there. Which means they occupy all the sofas and give saintly smiles that say, 'Too bad you've got to stand. In fact, I'm not even going to adjust a little bit, because I deserve a place for two.'

Next come their husbands. Who mostly look like they are caught between a vada pav and the chutney. They seem sheepish because they're wondering what's the correct protocol.

I'm not carrying a baby, so I should get up. But I'm next to the person who is carrying my baby, and I should be there for her, and it doesn't look like she's budging, and in fact she's giving me the side-eye that says don't you move darling, so maybe it will be okay if I continue to sit. But that other woman is glaring at me. Not side-eye, but full-frontal staring. But she's not pregnant. So, should I get up? Or should I ... wait, let me not make eye contact and start frantically messaging someone.

And then come other sundry people like mothers, sisters, cousins who are accompanying the pregnant person.

Last come the people standing outside the clinic in work clothes, talking into their phones.

And of course, the assistants who take your history don't make it easier.

'No children? At forty-four? After being married for so many years?'

Before they can give you that oh-poor-thing look, you rush in to tell them it's by choice. That you like kids, but you don't really want your own. That your nieces and nephews are your own. That the world has too many mouths to feed. As you blabber through the whole list, you see that pitying look being replaced by a cold stare. The one that says, 'You better stand outside and wait. No sofa for you, lady.'

I went back to the reception area and suddenly there was a flurry of excitement. The doctor had arrived. Files were shuffled, the assistant ran in and out, the usual crowd of people at the door started to form. Yes, these are those folks who think everyone else is an idiot; all you have to do is rush and stand outside the door, and every time it opens you'll fall in and hurrah, you'll beat everyone else who is waiting.

The crowd was dispersed. The receptionist went from bored to stern. The pregnant ladies had stopped fanning themselves, and were being called in one by one.

And then, I heard my name.

I grinned at Anirban and Oinx. Politely and firmly told them no one needs to come into the chamber with me. This is routine stuff, let me just get done with it. And before they could answer or protest, I was in.

The doctor was a nice elderly lady. She looked at my case history. And said, 'Let's do an examination.'

I went to the adjoining room, took off my T-shirt, and lay on the bed. She came, examined me, and asked me when I had noticed the lump. I answered but I started to blabber. This always happens to me. Put me in a dentist's chair, in a fancy gym, or in a salon with the hairdresser holding a pair of scissors next to me, and I start to blabber. Anything that scares me turns me into a grinning lunatic. And I'll be like, 'Chop it off' or 'Yes, take all those teeth off'. And all these people will think, wow, she's so cool and accommodating.

I'm not. I'm just so freaked out that everything's short-circuited. And I'm a hysterical wreck that can't stop words from gushing out of her mouth. That's how I once had my hair burned by a very incompetent hairdresser, and all I did was laugh and wave it off, while I was crying inside. That's also the reason why I probably hold the

world record for the number of years I've worn adult braces. I'd grin
my head off as my orthodontist stared down my mouth and tinkered
with my teeth. All my friends were convinced he was in love with me,
and that's why the treatment was taking so long. But I'm convinced
he thought I was in love with him, because I just couldn't stop smiling
my face off whenever I saw him.

Anyway, back to the gyneac's examination bed, where I am
blabbering on about my nipple, and how it's gone in. I can see her
eyebrows start to go up. She asks me, 'How long has it been since it's
gone in?' I take a deep breath and mumble, 'A while, I guess.' Actually,
I don't know. And I start describing how I've been wondering if it
will just pop back up and how every day when I have a bath, I'm
wondering what to do about it. She's looking at me so funny that I'm
beginning to wonder if she's going to slap me into my senses.

Obviously, that's not true. She's raising her eyebrows because she
is worried. But the more her eyebrows go up, the more I talk. It's like
my mind is frantically running around, shutting out all possibilities
of anything being wrong, while my mouth motors on.

She tells me to wear my T-shirt and come out. I'm waiting to hear
the words 'benign lump'. She hasn't airily dismissed me yet.

Maybe she'll do it now.

She asks me to sit. I stare at the countless gods displayed on
the table behind her. And start getting worried. If a doctor needs
so many gods, then I am in trouble. Is she hoping they'll help her
diagnose things better? Or are they an 'in case of emergency, break
glass' measure? When she can't understand what's wrong with you,
she hands you an idol.

Luckily, she hands me a sheet with a drawing of my boobs, and
something written on it, and says, 'I'm referring you for a sonomammography. It's probably nothing. But I'd like you to get the lump
checked because it's very big.'

I nod, say 'okay' and rush out. I'm already late for work, and the traffic is going to be terrible.

As I make a pit stop to pay at the counter, the receptionist says she's making the appointment for me for the sonomammography with a particular doctor at this big diagnostic clinic close by. I'm a little puzzled. Why the rush? She looks at me and says the doctor insisted. I shrug.

My appointment is fixed for two days later.

I leave the clinic telling Anirban and Oinx that she says it's nothing, but she still wants to run some more tests. What a bore. I get into my Uber, and that's when it strikes me. She never used the words 'benign lump'. I pull out my phone and WhatsApp my friend Ziba, who also has a history of benign lumps.

Me: Yo Ziba, doctor says mostly fibroid only, but it's very big. Sonography on Thursday.

Ziba: Mine was very big too. And was fibrocystic only. Don't worry.

Me: Yay!

2
ω

The next two days were a blur.

Not because I was worried about the lump. But because I was working my ass off.

This is where I officially declare my dirty secret to the world.

I was a workaholic.

And honestly, I have no idea how that happened. It's like a tub of salted caramel ice cream. You're walking past the refrigerator, you stop. Just one bite before you go watch some Netflix. You open the freezer, take out the tub, dig in, and put the spoon in your mouth. And are about to put the tub back in the freezer.

About to being the operative phrase. Because the next thing you know you're carrying the tub to the bed, thinking I'll just have a couple of bites while watching a whodunit on Netflix. And I'll have slow bites, so I savour it, and don't overdo it.

Season 3 of the whodunit gets over, and you're feeling slightly sick and super disgusted with yourself because you have no self-control. And there's hardly any ice cream left in the tub. You get up to keep it back, and ask yourself, who keeps that tiny bit of ice cream back? It'll just lie there for two years until mould starts growing out of it.

So, you eat the rest, and lick the sides. And quickly go to sleep before you can face yourself.

I was exactly like that.

One minute I was enjoying my job but also doing a million other things. And the next minute, boom, it was all over. I was working about twelve hours a day. Twelve hours in an office and twenty-four hours on the phone.

There have been times when on my way home after a long day, I've parked my car to the side of the road and wailed. Loud wails of helplessness. Then I've wiped my tears and gone on to take yet another call.

It's like that ice cream tub. You hate it, you hate yourself for not having any control, and yet you just can't stop.

So instead of worrying about how my life could change, true to habit, I spent the next two days worrying about deadlines and client meetings and creative work.

Aah, this is also probably a good time to tell you I work in advertising. And yes, for all of you who think advertising is super glam, let me tell you it's about as glam as an ulcer in the stomach that makes you want to puke all the time. I love it. But the pressures are enormous. And again, I'm not sure why. All we're doing is selling stuff. Not saving lives.

But the killer in my case was not just advertising.

It was that dirty, misused word: entrepreneurship.

Seriously, this is a ship I would ask no one to ever sail on. You are just so much better off working for someone. Because you have the right to say, 'I'm sorry, I can't do it.' Or 'I forgot', or 'I had a hangover', or 'My _____ (insert mother/father/fiancé/whatever) was ill'. When it's your own thing, that right is snatched away from you, and you turn around and realize you are where the buck stops. Scary place to be.

The last ten years of my life have been like that. Especially the last seven. It's been hectic, mad, and yes, a lot of fun. But towards the end of it, I could feel myself beginning to mentally and physically burn out. The last six months, I would come home at 9 p.m. Answer calls and check mails till 11 p.m. Somehow stuff my face with dinner, without even caring what I was eating. Drop off to sleep in front of the TV. Get up in the middle of the night to drink water or pee, and check my mail again.

And this was just the tip of the iceberg.

In fact, I think cancer probably saved my life. But I'll come back to that.

So, the two days flew past. I had told some folks in the office that there was a slight scare, but most probably it was nothing to worry about. Actually, what most probably? For sure this was nothing to worry about. I had a huge list of things to take care of, and this was definitely not pencilled in.

Breast cancer was so off my radar that it didn't even pop up in my brain. I was just irritated about the bother of taking a morning off. I think my brain was operating in a zero IQ zone. So instead of running to google 'nipple gone in', I was running for meetings. And brainstorming sessions, and revenue discussions, and profit and loss conversations.

Finally, the day arrived.

9.20 a.m.

Oinx: When are you going for your tests? Want me to come?
Me: 11 a.m.
Oinx: I am in no hurry to reach office.
Me: No. There's nothing for anyone to do there.

Oinx: Arre, I know. But I can come with you if you want.

Me: I just have to show up there. And it'll be done in 15 mins I am guessing.

I was cranky. An ex-colleague of mine, Manish, was in town. He and his wife have a travel company. And we had been talking about a possible collaboration between his company and mine. Today was supposed to be our first meeting. They lived in Delhi but were in Mumbai for three days. And after months of trying to get them and my partner, Parag, together, I had finally managed to pull it off. And they were going to spend the day at our office, figuring out how we could do some exciting stuff together.

I had been looking forward to it. We had many ideas, and this was the first time we were all going to sit with them, face to face.

I texted Manish and his wife, Shilpi, the night before, saying there's been a small hitch, but I'll be done in an hour max. And anyway, I had an early appointment, so we could just start at 12.30 instead of 11.30.

Ha! I was Jon Snow. I knew nothing.

I hated going to the office late. I hated doctor's appointments. I hated the fact that after all this planning, I'm going to be pushing our meeting by an hour.

Anirban was going to take time out from work and come to the diagnostic clinic as well. I hated that he had to take time off too.

So with my grumpy face, I head to the diagnostic centre. I have been told by the gynaec to meet a Dr Shilpa Lad. I haven't even bothered to google her, I don't really care who she is as long as she quickly checks my lady lumps and sends me on my way.

With an 'I got this' air, I walk in. The first floor is normal. Big TV screens tuned to a news channel, airline-style chairs for people to wait, some posters, and a registration counter.

By the way, who decides the channel to be played at these places? And why is it always the news? My theory is, they play the news at places like this to soften you up. Think of it like a barbeque. Before you actually make it to the tandoor, they'll marinate you. The news is never good. You'll sit there and stare at some of the bleakest things. Anchors screaming about murder, kidnapping, buildings falling, dramatic graphics that scare the life out of you, and everything in big, jarring text. Just when you are hypnotized and staring at every pixel popping out of that screen, they'll send you off to your tests. Now if the verdict is bad, you're already a shivering wreck who's expecting the worst from the world. Perfect.

I tell them I have an appointment for a sonomammography, and they say I have to go to the floor above.

I skip up the stairs and open the door. This room is exactly like the one below. But something is different. I give my name at the reception, fill a form, and look around. Dr Shilpa Lad is a leading breast cancer radiologist, says a poster with her name and bio.

Really? Ohkaaay then.

A tiny little voice is unfurling in my brain. Like a seed, there's an idea that's taking root. But I'm not paying any attention to it. Because, well, I am late for work. And seeds are something I eat with my morning smoothie.

The posters are all pink in colour, and talk about breast cancer. The statistics, the checking for lumps, the mammogram machine benefits. I look at all of them in passing.

I'm on the breast cancer floor in this centre. And I'm so not meant to be here. Because mine is only a routine test. And could they please just hurry it up.

I text Parag.

12.20 p.m.

Me: Hey. Sorry. This is taking time. I'm going to be late.
Parag: No worries, all well?

Me: I don't know yet. The walls are full of breast cancer statistics and posters.

Parag: Don't worry, it'll be nothing. Order lunch for you? Want ice cream?

I look at the people around. No one is really making eye contact. I'm dying to jump up and tell the lady at the reception to move it and show some speed, but instead I check my mail.

Anirban arrives. I grumble and tell him it's taking ages. He's looking at the walls as well, and is quiet.

It's difficult to describe what it felt like. I think it was an out-of-body experience. One day you are grinning and making plans, and the next day you are sitting in a room filled with posters on breast cancer. How is your brain supposed to process that?

And you have no symptoms, you eat right, you exercise, you love what you do. You have no reason to ever imagine you would be sitting here.

But there we were, looking into our phones. Unsure, a little worried, but not being able to say anything.

They call my name.

And a lady nurse tells me they'll do my mammography first, and then the sonography. I couldn't care less. They could do it in any combination they want and even throw in an autobiography, as long as they let me out quickly.

I follow her to a freezing room, where there is a big machine. The nurse asks me to take off my T-shirt and bra.

I, of course, have worn my nicest bra.

Yep, that's what I always do. First, I love bras. Second, they cost the earth. I have no idea why a piece of cloth and some lace and some wire could cost a fancy meal for two. But they do. And third, when there is a chance that you will take off your top, you must be wearing your best bra. Even if it is only for a nurse who is blinking at the neon bra you are now flashing.

Once the clothes are off, I am made to stand next to the machine. And the nurse, with this most matter-of-fact manner, takes one of my boobs and lifts it and squishes and wrestles with it. I'm watching, equally aghast and amused.

I mean, what does she fill in the job description paragraph?

Anyway, after much manoeuvring and squishing and lifting and muttering from the nurse, my boob is pressed against two plates. The two plates are stuck together really, really tight. It's worse than standing in the Mumbai local during rush hour. And of course, you are standing rather awkwardly, glued to the machine, one boob clamped, not allowed to move even an inch. At this point I am thankful that I don't have a paunch. I don't know why, but I would have freaked out if my boob and my tummy had felt cold metal.

Anyway, after some ten minutes, she repeats the whole operation with my other boob. By now, I'm used to the grind. Yep, it's literally that. A grinder for your boobs.

The nurse is pretty happy and chatty, and tells me I'm the first person who hasn't complained and has grinned through the boob grinder. I, of course, don't tell her I have a manic grinning problem. And it's hurting so bad that there are bells going off in my head.

Another ten minutes and we are done. She tells me I can wear my clothes and come out.

Now I'm amused. And I am dying to tell everyone how ridiculously funny her job is.

I come out, and the lady in the reception tells me that I need to go to the waiting room outside the doctor's office. There's a patient inside, and then it's my turn. I'm positively happy now. I have a funny story, and things have picked up speed.

Anirban and I go and sit in the waiting room. It has sofas and armchairs. And very thin walls. I can hear the doctor talking inside. And suddenly I feel that familiar ball of fear starting to unfurl in my tummy. I gulp it down.

A lady comes out, and the doctor calls my name.

I step into a dark room. There's a large monitor with some X-ray-like images. Possibly of my mammogram. And another large monitor in front of which sits an assistant, who is busy typing something.

The doctor smiles at me, and says, 'Hello Shormistha, let's get started.'

The nurse ushers me into a small changing room. I take off the T-shirt and the bra for the second time, clutch the sheet she gives me, and proceed to go out and lie on the narrow bed, right next to the sonography machine. The doctor rolls up on her stool, chats with me about how old I am and what symptoms I have. I start telling her everything I told the gynaec.

I am subdued now. It's like being in a giant exam hall, and your whole life will depend on this one viva question. Suddenly you worry that you are unprepared. For even the easiest question.

She's put the jelly on my breast, the left one, the one that has the lump. My arm is over my head. She's moving a joystick-like thing all over. And it's hurting. I'm gritting my teeth as I hear her talk to the assistant. Something about a cyst at 11 o'clock. And slowly I start to exhale. This is familiar stuff. It'll be over in no time. I've heard those words before.

Just then she slows down. And moves the joystick over a spot again. And again.

And mutters to herself, 'That's peculiar.'

And in that instant, I know.

Don't ask me how I knew. But the words and her tone, the signs that I had been ignoring, and the gynaec's expression on seeing my nipple, everything just whirled and clicked in a second. And I knew this was not going to be good.

But I was calm. Again, don't ask me how. I watched her continue the examination as she kept speaking to her assistant.

She put away the joystick. I could tell from her face. I wiped the jelly off, and she asked me to go and wear my clothes.

I calmly wore my bra and T-shirt. And stepped out and asked her, 'Should I call my husband in?'

She said yes.

That was it. They opened the door to call him, and he walked in. His face was still. Like he had been holding his breath.

We both looked at each other. The doctor asked us to sit. Him on a round stool, me on the edge of the bed that she had examined me on.

I don't remember her exact words because I felt like I was in a tunnel. Getting sucked into it fast. But I was breathing, and I knew she was looking at him and saying, 'It doesn't look good, and we should get a biopsy done.'

Both of us looked at each other again. We had no idea what to do, how to react. My mind was moving in slow motion. Everything was very clear, but happening very slowly. She understood. She's probably seen patients go into that kind of shock. Where you just can't comprehend what is being said.

She made the decision for us, saying, 'Let me speak to your gynaec. I could do the biopsy here in the next two days. Or maybe she'll want to speak to you.'

We both sat there, in the dark, with the glow of the monitor falling on our faces. Very silent. While she called the doctor and told her that the result didn't look good, she was worried and I needed a biopsy.

The gynaec told her to send us back to her.

The doctor looked at us and very gently said, 'I am so sorry. Your gynaec has asked you to meet her immediately.'

We nodded, said thank you, took the file she handed us, and walked out. Into the bright waiting room. I walked over to where my shoes were, Anirban by my side. And I looked at him.

And burst into tears.

He held me. I could feel that he was crying as well. And we both just stood there, holding on for dear life as we let the news wash over us.

3

I was waiting. Sitting on the sofa and waiting outside the doctor's chamber.

Initially, I was okay, checking my phone and stuff.

And the thing is, you can hear everything that's happening inside the chamber.

There was one point when I heard her say, 'One second, one second, go over that again.'

I remember the words very distinctly.

And then there was a word she used, and I was on Google immediately.

She said there's something of something there. And that word just sounded scary to me.

And I immediately googled it, and that was it. I was half zoned out by the time they called me, and I walked in.

I kind of knew before I walked in. Not really knew-knew, but something was off.

I had heard her say that's peculiar, and then she used that other word. The moment she said it, I was fearing the worst.

Not what it would be, my mind was not putting it into words. I was just very afraid.

—*Anirban*

4

(ധ)

It's funny.

I don't remember the word she used. Apart from peculiar.

Now when I think back, I remember that she checked my right breast first. It was probably closer to her. And I remember her slowly and methodically checking, and talking to her assistant.

It's only when she came to the left breast, I started hearing words like calcification. And my mind started to go blank.

But today, as I write this, I checked her report to find the word Anirban heard.

And it was metastatic.

And it comes from the Latin word 'metastasis' which means transition.

Well, little did I know how much of a transition I had waiting for me. My whole life was going to change, forever.

We walked out of the diagnostic clinic. Anirban was holding the report in his hand. I was incapable of processing anything. We sat in the car, holding hands, in silence. It was a grey day in March. Cloudy, murky, and very dull. I remember looking out of the window and watching people go about their lives. While mine was in pieces.

I think I was numb.

It's like when you get hurt or you are in an accident, how everything just goes into slow motion. It felt exactly like that. Like I was watching a particularly gloomy foreign movie, the kind they show in film festivals, black and white, shot in slo-mo, where I was the main lead.

Me: Oinx, they have some worries about the test. So, they have recommended a biopsy. Have come back to the doctor.

Oinx: Oh god! Is Anirban with you?

Me: Yes he is.

Oinx: Ok. Don't worry. It will be all good. In a meeting. Calling you in a bit.

We reached the gyneac's building. There were people waiting. I walked up to the receptionist and told her I had just done my mammo, and the gyneac wanted to meet me. She asked me to wait and went into the chamber.

We sat there. Staring into space. Holding hands.

And then the receptionist comes out and calls my name.

In slow motion, I see myself enter the room. The gyneac looks worried. I sit down. Anirban hands her my file.

It's a slim file. What I don't know is that the file is going to get thicker and thicker as the year goes by. It's going to be stuffed with reports and examinations, and biopsy reports and lab tests, and blood tests and PET scans and MRIs.

It's going to be the first signal to attendants, nurses, doctors, and other patients that I have cancer.

Every time I walk into a hospital, that file will be my identity. And for months that is all I will be. A thick bunch of reports and files and X-rays and prescriptions and everything else that I could never have imagined.

The gynaec looks up, removes her glasses, and says, 'I am so sorry. This is beyond what I can do. I think the best thing for you to do is consult an oncologist.'

My mind is so far away that for two minutes I'm just staring at her, wondering why she wants me to see an eye doctor.

I hear Anirban start to talk to her. I'm still staring. My brain is trying to work it out. And then it strikes me. Oncologist. Not ophthalmist.

She wants me to see a cancer doctor.

How could that be possible? I don't know anyone who has cancer. Or has had cancer. I don't know any oncologists. How does one find one? And where do they sit? I've hardly ever been to a hospital.

I feel helpless and lost.

Anirban is looking at me. I try to focus on what she just said.

'The best thing to do is see an oncologist. The sooner the better. We can do a biopsy, but it'll take time for the results. And I don't think you should wait. In this case, we are always worried about too much too soon, or too little too late. An oncologist will be able to guide you, without wasting any time.'

We are both looking at her.

And then it probably strikes her, how lost we look.

She continues, 'Don't worry. I can recommend a good oncologist. He sits thrice a week at Hinduja in Mahim. Should I call him and try to get an appointment?'

I don't know what makes me say no.

But the fog lifts for a bit. And I say no loudly.

In my head I see a hospital corridor, and in the room in the end, an elderly doctor. Balding. White coat. Waiting.

But he's not the one for me.

The gynaec looks surprised at my loud no. So does Anirban.

But I've decided. I want to go to my family GP and ask him what to do.

I want comfort. I want someone I can trust.

The gynaec looks sorry for me. I can tell looking at her that it's not good news. The biopsy is probably a formality. And she genuinely looks distressed for us.

I tell her that I want to go to my GP. She nods. She probably realizes that it'll take time for the news to sink in. We pick up the file, say thank you, and leave. She wishes me all the best.

And that's the other thing. I have to start getting used to people looking at me with a sorry face. And wishing me luck.

I know everyone means well. But there's just a lot of 'looking at me with a sorry face' coming up, and at this moment I have no idea how to deal with it.

We step outside and for the first time we speak. I look at Anirban and I tell him that I want to check with Dr Ramchandani, or Chandu, as we call him with easy familiarity. Anirban nods. His face is pale. He tells me that we'll do just that.

Chandu is the neighbourhood GP, who has a clinic down the road from my house. He has silver hair, he knows my name, he knows I get hay fever. His receptionists are my friends. For some reason, I want him to tell me what to do. Not some doctor who I meet once in two years for a sonography.

And at that point I don't think I have the strength to meet an oncologist. It's just too much for a single day. I need time to process this, I need advice from those I can trust.

As we sit in the car and go towards Chandu's clinic, I watch Anirban from the corner of my eye. He's still holding my hand. But he looks so sad.

It's funny. There is no loud proclamation of 'don't worry', or 'we'll fight this together', or any such thing. There's just a dazed feeling.

Both of us giving each other time to process this, before we decide how we'll deal with it.

We instinctively hold hands, and it's like a piece of a puzzle that just fits. We've been going through a rough time, in our marriage and our friendship. And today, without a word being said, we just slide back to being what we were.

We reach the clinic. It's already 2 p.m. Barely any people around, which is super rare. Anirban goes and talks to the receptionist. The receptionist looks worried and nods. I nod back, composing my face to look sad as well. Though honestly, I don't know how I should look. Or react.

We wait.

And slowly, my head starts to clear. I was sinking, but I feel like I've touched the bottom of the ocean. And it's calm. I can see light filtering in, far, far away. But in my head, as I sit cross-legged on the ocean floor, looking at the patterns on the sand, and light and shadow, I start feeling calm. And my control freak nature starts to kick in.

Before we go further, a little bit about me.

I have always been this 'not just glass half-full person', but also 'seize the chance to add some Old Monk to it' kind of person.

It's a massive advantage, but in some situations, it can also be really difficult.

Because I can never really accept defeat. I will do everything under the sun to better a situation, to fix it, to come out on top.

And there are times when you can do everything possible, and it will still not go your way. Those are the times I am crushed.

I have no idea and no skills to deal with that.

The fight in me starts to kick in. Slowly, but it's alive. I can feel it.

And I realize I need to take control, of myself, and whatever it is that I have.

We get called into the doctor's chamber.

He is standing up, the receptionist has probably whispered in his ear. Anirban hands him the file. He looks at it. There's no smile, no 'So how are you, Shormistha?', nothing.

He says exactly what the gyneac said.

'You should see an oncologist.'

That feeling of helplessness is flooding back into my system. This is the doctor I trust the most. He can fix anything. How is he saying there's nothing he can do?

He continues, 'The best place to go to is Tata Memorial. They are the best. Everyone from all across the country goes there. My wife has been there as well. Get an appointment and see the oncologist.'

There's nothing else to be done.

The receptionist says she's sorry to hear the news. I nod.

We walk out, and down the lane, to the gate of our building.

Anirban asks me what I want to do.

I've decided. I want to go to work.

I want everything to be familiar and happy. I don't want to sit lost and miserable at home.

I want to put this dreary, cloudy, grey day behind me. Also, I want time to be by myself. And the commute to the office will help.

I decide to take an Uber.

Uber is my comfort ride. Like dal, chawal aur Uber.

There's something about sitting in the back of a cab, staring out of a window, chatting with the driver if you feel like it, making a cab office. It's like a train compartment. You can hang your bag and pull out your book, air pillow, water bottle, and make it home for the next twenty-four hours or so.

Uber is similar. It takes me forty minutes from home to the office. And my laptop, my bag, my jacket, my mid-morning snack litters the back seat. I think about the day, what I need to do next, friends I need to call back, checking on my parents who live in Delhi.

So, I call a cab. And Anirban says he'll go to office too.

He tells me he'll start finding out who to meet and how to meet, at Tata Memorial.

I'm so hungry. It's about 2.30 p.m. now. Way past my lunchtime. My stomach is growling. And I want to shut this out. I want to forget about it.

I nod. Hug him tight, jump into a cab, and leave for work.

When I think back, I think some of it was me hoping it would go away if I got into a car and disappeared.

I wanted to put it aside. This was the worst day in my life. And every cell in my body was telling me that if I ignore it, it would be fine.

We're going down the Western Express Highway in Mumbai. I'm staring at all the billboards. I've never been to the office this late; the traffic is light, it looks like a holiday. Or like everyone's fled on hearing the news.

Oinx is in a meeting. I message her. Tell her it doesn't look good.

I message Parag, tell him the same thing. And that I'm on my way to work.

Then the phone rings. It's my aunt, calling from America. Out of the blue.

Growing up, I hardly knew my aunt. My dad was in the Air Force and we lived in places whose names you could barely pronounce, forget finding on the map. My aunt moved to America early in her life. So, we barely ever met.

Till one day, when I was thirty-two and going to Italy on a work trip. I think Dad told my aunt that I was travelling to Europe alone, and planning to do a solo trip after my meetings. My aunt called me, again out of the blue, saying she'd join me, because this was her chance to get to know me and make up for all the lost time.

I was sold.

I look at my phone as her number flashes, I take the call, and say hi.

And before she can say anything, I blurt out, 'I've been asked to see a cancer doctor. They think I have breast cancer.'

You know how they talk about the universe working in mysterious ways. Well, this was one of those things. Why would the universe choose to make this aunt call me, over all the people in the world?

Because she is as cool as gin and tonic.

She took the news calmly, said oh damn a couple of times. Asked me everything. And told me not to worry till the doctor's told me I have something to worry about.

Just listening to her being normal and calm started to make me feel better. It wasn't even a very long call, or full of sympathy or anything like that. We just discussed it normally, she was feeling bad that I might have breast cancer and that was it.

By the time I reached office, I was feeling way better.

Famished. But way better.

I walked into the office. A bunch of anxious faces looked over their screens at me. Parag knew. Manish and his wife as well. And two or three other people, who knew why I was coming in late. They were waiting.

I warmed the lunch they had ordered for me, and spoke to them in a little huddle at the pantry area. I was on familiar territory. I felt comforted, brave even.

I think everyone took it well. Or like me, they didn't understand the extent of what was coming. Of course, they were worried, and immediately everyone was online trying to book appointments at Tata Memorial. I remember laughing and telling them to chill, 'We'll do this aaram se.'

That's also a problem with me. Left to myself I would have probably taken two months to get an appointment. I would have gone online, got bored halfway through filling the form, and started shopping on Amazon. When it comes to handling stuff like forms, reports, or taxes, I am the worst.

I tell Parag, Manish, and Shilpi that I'll think about all this later. Let's get to work.

I remember sitting on the floor in the conference room, talking and laughing, and convincing myself that it will be all okay.

The phone pings. It's Anirban. He's found someone who knows an oncologist at Tata Memorial. That too, a breast cancer specialist.

What? How did he do this? Okay, he's far more capable than me, but this is too much.

I call him back immediately. Turns out someone in his office is friends with the oncologist, and her sister. I have setting. Hurrah.

I'm going to interrupt everything here, to say thank you to Manisha. Again, it was like a sign. Like the universe just planted someone who could help us. Make it a little easier when we were so lost.

That said, it makes you wonder what it's like if you don't know anyone. If you don't have any kind of setting. I'll tell you what. It makes you extremely thankful for what you have.

And that's what I felt. Not destroyed that I have cancer. But grateful, that I have people who love me, the means, friends, a job where everyone is supportive.

I wasn't unlucky. I was lucky.

5

ᗺᗺ

When I look back at that day, there are a couple of things that stick out in my head.

One is the sense of relief that flooded through my body as I held on to Anirban and cried. It's crazy. Who feels that? But while I felt awful and scared, I also felt like someone had taken a huge weight off my shoulders.

The last couple of years had been troubled, in my head. If you met me or hung out with me, you'd never know. Not even those closest to me will know, but I was a mess. Okay, fine, I was a hot mess.

On the surface I had everything. Yet, there were things that gnawed at me. Maybe it was a midlife crisis, maybe I didn't know where I was headed. I wanted to work, I didn't want to work, I loved having my own company, I hated having my own company, I was happily married, I was unhappily married, I was fine, I was not fine. I didn't know which one I was. And I was running away from it all. By throwing myself into my work with reckless abandon. It got to a point where I hated it, and also hated myself, but I just couldn't stop.

A couple of months before I got diagnosed, I was driving back home, and a thought popped into my head. *What if I fell ill? What if something major happened to me? That would be the perfect way to stop this crazy roller coaster I was on.*

I think I scared myself. It was scary. Like I was willing something bad to happen to me, so I could take control of my life. Ha! The irony.

A giant warning bell that had been ringing in my head for a while suddenly started buzzing loudly. That night, I got home, washed my face (Yep, always wash your face when you want to talk to yourself. Remember, best face forward and all that), and spoke to myself. I really needed to fix my life.

I didn't make a complete U-turn, but I was on my way to going back to what I had been. I started with my diet. I met the most amazing nutritionist. I was eating healthy after a long time, cooking meals, feeling happy in my tummy. I spent a long holiday with my parents in Goa. Doing nothing, but swimming and drinking feni and driving them around every afternoon. I started spending time with Anirban and realized how much I had missed his company. My mind was just beginning to filter out the rubbish and bring me to a happy place … when bam! You go see an oncologist, lady!

I think about that moment a lot. Where on the one hand I was howling my head off scared to death. And on the other hand, a tiny voice in my head was jumping up and down, telling me this was my chance to change my life. That U-turn that I was slowly taking, this was the moment when I could step on the accelerator. When I could just throw away all the rubbish and all the frustration, and start afresh.

This wasn't just a visit to a therapist or a nutritionist, this was my chance to walk through fire and come out a new person.

I know it sounds a bit like a Sanjay Leela Bhansali movie right now. Hair flying in the wind, temple bells ringing, Good Earth curtains fluttering in a sudden breeze, I raise my head and look into Anirban's eyes and say in a slow sexy voice with just a hint of a tremble, 'There is nothing stronger than a strong woman.'

But nothing like that happened. I was dribbling snot over his shirt and shitting myself in fear. While that little voice was being so extra, yelling, 'Think of this as your big chance, girl.' And strangely, that voice was getting through to me. Giving me hope.

The second thing that sticks out in my head is when the radiologist, the gyneac, and the GP broke the news, not once did it cross my mind: Why me?

What worried me were the practicalities.

How on earth will I find an oncologist? Where do people go for that? No one in my family is a doctor. Shit, I don't have any setting.

I think being middle class and worrying about setting saved my ass. It broke it down into things that I could actually fret about and figure out how to tackle. Rather than the more existential, metaphysical, spiritual (insert all other big words ending with 'al') question, 'Why me?'

Again, when you are an optimist, your brain believes that there is a solution to every problem. And dismisses those questions that it knows there's no figuring out. There is no answer, no hack, no way to conclude a question like 'Why me?', so why even go there.

Instead, I was like, 'Why now?' Just when I was losing weight and looking hot. Or just when I had discovered my cycling legs and was doing 100 kms a week. Or just when I had plans to go for a wedding. Why now?

I'm a serial wedding bunker. So, the last one was big for me.

Actually, I'm not an intentional bunker. What happens is I'm usually super excited about attending a wedding, especially an out-of-town one. So, in my head I'll plan everything out, outfit, jewellery, matching shoes. Rest of the clothes, gift, etc. And I'll discuss, make lists, buy tickets, tie up with other friends to go together. And then by the time it's the day I have to depart for the wedding, I am exhausted. With all the planning and thinking in my head. I've already been to the wedding, eaten the food, and taken a selfie on the stage. And it is super boring.

Then I just bunk.

Only reason I'm explaining this is because a lot of my friends who hopefully will buy this book, well, I haven't been to their weddings.

I love you guys. Tell you what, get married again. I'm a changed woman.

Oh, and some more things.

My radiologist was lovely. She was worried but gentle. This is the first time I had ever gone to her, but she radiated empathy. And she asked me if I wanted her to do a biopsy. She was ready to act.

The gyneac and my GP, they were equally nice to me. However, I felt like I was a case for them now. A cancer case. So, it was best to give me the right advice and tell me to quickly go to the oncologist. There was no reaching out to me, no telling me not to worry. I know they can't do that as doctors. But it's hard when the people who first inform you are the ones who can't do anything at all. You feel lost. Like I did that day.

And the silence. I'm a person who loves to talk things out. I don't do silence. If you're ill or mad at me or anything at all, I'll badger you to talk to me. That's how bad I like to fix things.

But that day I couldn't talk. It was all in my head, like a cupboard where clothes are just jumbled and thrown in, and you're scared to open it in case they tumble out and drown you.

It was like that. All the thoughts running through my head. Practical thoughts, scared thoughts, that voice that was jumping up and down, everything at the same time.

But I couldn't utter anything.

I couldn't find the words. And I couldn't tell Anirban my head was running riot.

Thankfully, he isn't like me. And he let me stay silent. While he processed stuff as well.

I think those couple of hours of silence set the tone for how it would be between us. Non-hysterical, no forced cheer, no we'll survive. We'll just hold hands, and take it as it comes.

6

The rest of the day passed quickly in office. Those who knew what was up with me got to work. Trying to book me an appointment online. Which believe me is tougher than trying to find a good sari blouse tailor.

I was laughing at them, and telling them to chuck it. Told you, I am that person who just puts off anything important. Especially when it comes to filling forms. Forms and me, we have history. If I kept a record of the number of forms I've filled halfway and abandoned, we could build ourselves a tiny forest.

But this was reassuring. Just to be surrounded by people who cared. Who were not weeping and freaking out. At least not to my face. And who were trying to figure how they could help.

Between fending questions, and making plans with Manish and Shilpi, my mind was busy. And then Anirban called saying he'd got us an appointment.

I quickly told my colleagues to call off the hunt for an online appointment. I was meeting the oncologist tomorrow at 9 a.m. So, no office for me.

Note: I was still using the word oncologist. Getting a feel of it in my mouth, wrapping my tongue around the syllables, and my mind around what it stood for. In a couple of months, I'd be using the abridged version of it, onco. Just tossing the word 'onco' around like croutons in a soup. It would roll off my tongue with the confidence of a person who had a super thick patient file.

Well, little did I know that I had popped my cancer cherry.

I think my colleagues were all a little worried. But for some reason, most of them were thinking this was just a scare. Maybe they didn't want to believe it. Or maybe they couldn't imagine it could happen to me. Me, who cycled, did yoga, ate properly. Me, who was full of life and exuberance.

I think it was the latter.

And even though no one said anything to me, their unsaid reactions and feelings were trickling into my consciousness. I was still making up my mind on how this would play out. Where did I stand? What is the course I would take?

Not the cancer. Or the oncologist. But me.

As Shormistha, how would I deal with this? And slowly, like when the clouds part just before you land and you see the runway, a picture was emerging in my head.

Of what I must do. How I must be.

Anirban messaged me, telling me he'd be home early. I think he knew I wouldn't want to be alone. So just like a regular day, I wound up my work, told my colleagues that I'll be gone tomorrow but would be back the day after, and grabbed an autorickshaw home.

I had the entire zoo waiting for me when I got home. Milo, my dog, immediately came and nuzzled me and sat on my lap and wanted petting. Just small everyday things that seem so huge on a night when you don't know what'll happen to your life the next day. I clung on to him, held him close.

Anirban had warmed our dinner. I ate, told him about my day. He told me about how he had gone to the office and told his colleagues about what the doctor said. And how one of them immediately said she knew someone in the breast cancer department at Tata Memorial. Next thing you know, she's made the call and she's got an appointment for 9 a.m.

Nine a.m. The first appointment of the day. Even more precious because we wouldn't have to wait. Something that immediately made me feel very privileged. But I would only realize the extent of that privilege when I went to the hospital the next day.

And the second reason the first appointment was so special was of course because we'd know. Straight off the bat. No waiting half a day and living with this thing. The irony being, I had been living with it for months and ignoring it. And suddenly all I wanted was to know. And to deal with it. Whatever it was.

I called Oinx and told her the plan for the next day. She said she was coming with us. No two ways about it. I tried hawing and humming, asking her not to come. But my heart wasn't in it. I knew I'd be glad for the company. And of course, she wasn't going to take no for an answer.

As I wound down for the day, I was just tired. Physically and mentally. Tuggu, the building cat that we had adopted, had also walked into the house by then, so I just gave myself up to being cuddled, and held by Anirban and the pets.

I slept like a log.

It's funny, usually I'm a light sleeper. Or I wake up a million times and go back to sleep. Or I have allergies, and I'll sneeze in the middle of the night and wake up. I'm most definitely not a 'slept like a log for eight hours, in one position' person.

But that night I was. In fact, for the next couple of days, as my diagnosis became clearer, and heavy cancer words like 'carcinoma' and 'invasive' started getting tossed around, the sounder I slept. Like my body was kicking in some defence mechanism. I would hit the pillow and promptly pass out. No staying awake in stress. No worrying. No nothing. Just engulfed in sleep.

Seems strange.

Let me tell you what's stranger.

My work gave me sleepless nights.

I hadn't slept as well in ages. I would toss and turn, and wake up a million times. Like an addict who needed a fix, I would reach out for my phone every time I tossed or turned. And once the phone glowed, my sleep just vanished. This glowing Aladdin's cave filled with job lists and client mails and world domination plans would suck me right in. And I'd be answering emails at 2.30 a.m. Or making a job list at 4 a.m.

It was unhealthy. And there was no one to blame but me.

I only realized that when my chemos had set in.

How could cancer and everything that came with it—the fear, the pain, the sickness, the loneliness, the uncertainty—how could that let me sleep soundly at night? Barring maybe a couple of nights.

And my work, how could it have been the opposite?

Was the way I was working worse than my cancer?

I have a theory for that. And I'll come back to it. But for now, on the first day of being told that I might have cancer, and that I needed to see an oncologist, I was sleeping like a baby.

The morning was rushed. You'd imagine we were going to work. Jostling for the loo, trying to grab breakfast. But it obviously wasn't like any other day, because there was a file lying on the table. And inside that, like a ticking Laxmi bomb, were the sonomammo reports. Oinx was picking us up, and then going to work. Lucky for me, she was on her notice period and could afford to come along.

I stuffed my face with breakfast. I was sticking to my healthy food. In fact, I had lost 3 kgs in the last two months, and was feeling lighter and brighter. It made me want to laugh, as I scarfed down my breakfast, that here I am at my healthiest weight, BMI, body fat, and I've been told I have breast cancer. I mean I'm fitting into small sizes, my jeans for once are falling off my hips, my stomach is like you ran a rolling pin over it, and I have cancer!

Oinx calls. She's waiting with her car downstairs. We leave the house. I'm looking around one last time. I don't know why. But I want to imprint the house and what normal looks like in my brain. Just remember it like that.

The phone pings.

> Ziba: You did your scan?
> Me: Hey did it. They saw something that worried them. Suggested a biopsy immediately. Went back to the doctor. Doctor said best to go to a cancer specialist and do everything under his/her guidance. So heading to Tata Memorial now. Have an appointment at 9.
> Ziba: Oh Shorms … is someone with you?
> Wishing and praying it will all be well. Hugs.
> Please keep me informed when possible.

Anirban and Oinx are chatting. Something about coffee and the food at the newly opened café near our house that we all love. I'm looking out of the window, absent-mindedly staring out, as I chat with them. It's another grey and gloomy day. The monorail that stretches over Parel dwarfs the road in its shadow. Again, I feel like I'm in a movie. And I'm watching this very bleak and hopeless city of the future from my window. And suddenly Google Maps shows us that we are at our destination.

Tata Memorial. The first time you get off, and you look at it, the only thing you really want to do is flee. The pavements outside and the driveway is lined with people, clutching those telltale files. You see patients, sitting, leaning, lying back, heads resting on shoulders, pipes in noses, blank eyes, hopeful eyes. Men, women, and the most heartbreaking thing ever, children. And those damn files. Thick, thin, carefully kept in large plastic packets that have the names of shops printed on them. From sari to sweet shops, reminders of happier times, those files are everywhere.

We get out of the car. I'm already so aware of how privileged I am as we drive up to the entrance. There are people sitting all over, some not being able to move, some overcome by weakness, taking a short break before they walk a few steps, and some waiting for a taxi or someone who can lend them a shoulder.

I feel all this, and I see all this.

We walk through the doors. Everyone walking in or out seems very purposeful. They know what's to be done. We have no idea.

There's a reception desk, but the person behind it is missing. We look for a signboard. The person arrives. We tell him we have an appointment, and he points us to the stairway. We need to go to the first floor.

The first floor is filled with light. It feels like a massive railway station. There are people everywhere. It doesn't seem as bleak as the outside because everyone is so focused. People are standing, crossing, moving. We ask at the counters set up in the massive hall, and are pointed in the direction of the breast cancer section.

As we walk towards it, the crowds increase. But it's early, and there's still some place to sit at the reception area outside the doctor's chambers.

I'm wearing my favourite blue pants. In fact, they are now loose on me. And an old T-shirt I like a lot. And my favourite purple canvas shoes. Again, little do I know that this will become a uniform for me. And I will wear it over and over again, for luck and for courage.

Oinx and I, we stand around. While Anirban goes to the reception. I'm mentally expecting a long wait. My eyes are taking everything in, but my mind is calm. I think, at some level, I already know the diagnosis.

To my surprise, in less than ten minutes, a head pops out of one of the chambers, and I hear my name being called. I walk into a hospital room after ages. The last time I was in one was when my dog bit my nose. And before you blame my dog, it was an accident. I was bored and he was sleeping on the bed. In a moment of being a complete dumb fuck, I put my face right next to him and let out a blood-curdling yell. He thought he was being attacked, I panicked, and in the bargain, there was a fountain of blood gushing out of my nose.

I remember racing around the house like a headless chicken. My brain told me coffee would stop the blood and so would ice, but the fountain of blood was blurring my vision and clouding my brain, because I took the coffee jar from the kitchen shelf and put it in the freezer. And then stood there waiting for the bleeding to stop.

Anyway, eventually I did manage to pull myself together and call Anirban. And get to the emergency room of the closest hospital.

After that rather eventful incident nine years back, this was my first time in a hospital room. It looked pretty standard, metal table, chairs. Stuff piled up. A young doctor sat behind the desk, paper and pen ready. He asked us the usual bunch of questions. This was the third round, once at the gyneac's, the second at the sonomammo, and now here. I was prepared.

44 years.

Married.

No children.

Noticed a lump.

Nipple had gone in.

No history of breast cancer in the family.

Grandmother had stomach cancer, as did my father's brother.

Smoke rarely. Not more than one cigarette.

Drink very occasionally.

Works out.

No other medical conditions.

Thank you.

The doctor wrote down everything.

Here's a question. Why do doctors not use a laptop or a computer to note this stuff? Why are they perpetually using sheets of paper? And mostly they hand them to you. And then you are stuck with safekeeping this weather-beaten sheet which has been scrawled all over, and you need to guard it forever. Which I am terrible at. Papers, documents, and me. We have a relationship that can be filed under Missing, or Careless, or Misplaced, or I forgot.

The doctor then took that sheet and went to the next room, while we waited. Was I scared? No. But it felt a bit like I was outside my body, watching this whole scene play out.

He popped his head back in and said the doctor will see us. We walked to the next chamber. A small room with a desk and light box. My sonomammo sheets were on it. There was also an examining table with a curtain, some chairs, and a large cabinet. And another young doctor was present.

The oncologist smiled when I walked in, and introduced herself and asked if she could examine me straight off. I nodded and walked towards the bed. The assistant doctor pulled the curtain, and I heard Anirban thank the onco surgeon for meeting us at such short notice.

She came to the examination table. I lay there, on the narrow cot, with my T-shirt and bra off. She asked me which breast I had felt the lump in. I said left. She started to examine me. And asked apart from the lump was there anything else I noticed. And I said yes, my nipple had completely gone in a couple of days earlier and I kept expecting it to pop up, but that wasn't happening. And I started getting worried. I saw her frown when I said that.

And while she examined my right breast, my mind started putting two and two together.

You bloody idiot, Shormistha. This is a sign. Nipple going in. Just folding inside by itself like a tantric yoga kriya, and you thought it's normal? What is wrong with you? Bas, now you are fucked.

She finished examining me in silence. I lay there staring at the ceiling, all these thoughts running through my head.

She stepped out, I wore my clothes. Slowly, lingering just a little longer than I should have. It's like I knew those were the last few seconds before everything would change.

I came out from behind the curtain. She was waiting for me. I sat down on the chair next to Anirban, and she said:

'Okay, I would rather just give it to you straight up. I'm sorry, but you have the disease.'

I nodded. She kept talking.

My mind and I were also talking,

Shormistha, you have cancer.

Yep, I know. I heard the lady. But listen, why did she call it the disease? Why didn't she use the word 'cancer'?

You have cancer.

Shit. I know. Actually, wait a minute, I knew this from yesterday. I'm kind of okay. Not really shocked.

Sure?

Yep.

Okay, then listen to what she's saying.

She was writing in a notepad while she spoke.

'Okay, so I'm writing it down because I'm sure you'll google it. (ha ha … she really didn't know me. Too lazy and spaced out to google anything.) There are two lumps. One we are not sure about. But the other one definitely is cancerous. There's also a lot of calcification. Doesn't look good.'

I watched her draw boobs on paper. As she circled the spots where my lumps were.

I looked at Anirban. He looked composed. I think he was holding my hand.

She kept speaking and writing on the notepad. Telling us that it could be a non-invasive breast cancer restricted to the milk ducts. Or it could have spread beyond. And gone to the tissue, and even the lymph nodes.

Milk ducts? What? I never thought of my boobs like that.

And lymph nodes. I've heard about lymph nodes but what do they do?

Then she paused. I think she realized we were both very silent. And she said, 'Look, we'll have to operate either way. Depending on what it is, we might have to do a lumpectomy, which is just removing the lump, or it could also be a mastectomy. Which means we'll have to remove the entire breast. And another thing, it looks like your lump is very close to the nipple. So, we might have to take a call to sacrifice the nipple.'

How do you describe a day where you are told that you have cancer? And that one part of your body, a part that defines you as a woman, will have to go?

I guess you'll call it a shit day.

Or a very shit day even.

But at that point, it's like someone had flipped a switch inside me.

I was calm. The calmest I've ever been. No tears, no hysterics, no why me, no how sad is my life.

The not crying part is strange. Because I cry at almost everything. I cry while watching those singing reality shows on TV. You know that bit when a contestant is selected, and gets a card from the judges. And then they play a slow-motion clip of the person running out of the room, pumping their fists. And their parents are crying. And the grandmother in the village is crying and hugging their photo. Well, guess who else is crying and hugging the remote.

When I was at school and *Qayamat Se Qayamat Tak* came out, I remember going to a friend's place to watch it. They were foreign-returned and had a VCR. My friend, who obviously knew what a sap I was and didn't want a bawling girl disturbing the peace in their house, stopped the movie just before the end. I had no idea how VCRs were operated, and grew up believing that *QSQT* was the sweetest love story with a rather abrupt ending. Some song was being sung, and that's it, it just ended there.

When I went to college, our hostel had movie nights on Friday. And the cultural committee decided to do a love story run for Valentine's Day. That night they played *QSQT*, and I learnt the truth. I cried so much that I brought the movie night to a halt, and had hiccups for a day.

But at that moment, as the oncologist spoke to me, I was floating in a haze of calmness.

She looked at us. I wonder now if she expected tears or hysterics. And if this slightly manic, grinning patient worried her.

'I know it sounds scary, but it's nothing, really. More than anything it's an inconvenience, an irritant. You'll have to go through things, and your life will be disrupted for some time. That's the part that'll be hard. Breast cancer is the most treatable form of cancer, you don't have anything to worry about.'

My out-of-body experience continued as I smiled and said thank you to her. And asked what the next steps are.

She said, 'We'll have to run tests to understand the extent of it. So, don't start stressing till you know what it is. Most importantly, you'll have to decide which doctor you want. If you are comfortable with me, then we'll start right now. Or if you want to go to another place, I could recommend my teacher. He is the head of the breast cancer department at Kokilaben Hospital. He's also a great doctor. And yes, if you can afford it and would rather go to a private hospital, then that's where you should go.'

I smiled from ear to ear. Remember what I told you. How my mind goes blank at the dentist's chair, or the hairdressers chair, and I grin my head off and say, 'Do whatever you have to.' Or when there's a yoga pose that's killing me, and I'm dying inside, I'll just be grinning more and more as it absolutely wipes me out.

So, I grin and tell her, 'I like you. You be my doctor.'

I think she was a little taken aback. I don't know if it was my enthusiasm for having her as my doctor or just my grinning. But she recovered fast and said, 'Great. Then let's get an MRI done first thing.'

She scribbles more stuff on that tiny paper and hands it to me.

I'm freaked out. Damn, am I going to have to keep this paper safe, and for how long?

Thankfully, Anirban calmly takes it. We say thank you and tumble out of the room.

There's no time to think. Oinx is waiting, with big questioning eyes. The place has filled up. I manage to get close to her and I tell her it's cancer. She looks stricken. Anirban and I fill her in on the details.

We walk to the reception. I'm assuring Oinx I'm fine. I'm just glad to have Anirban and her with me.

While Anirban fills the forms at the reception, my fog starts to clear, thanks to the fact my middle-class behaviour is never too far away, and is always ready to kick in.

Money. This is going to cost money.

And I have medical insurance.

Hallelujah!!!

Seriously, never have I been more pleased with myself. If I could, I would have hugged myself.

Two years back, I decided that it was ridiculous that I was over forty and didn't have any medical cover. So, I got myself a Mediclaim policy. And get this, I also got a critical illness policy that covers a variety of scary diseases, including the one that I had just been diagnosed with.

I lean against the counter and make a call to my insurance guy. Who picks up on the second ring. I tell him what the scene is, and how I've just been told that it is breast cancer. And will he help me? Will my insurance cover it? He's awesome. He tells me to worry about my health and getting better, and he'll make sure it's all covered and I'm okay.

My manic grin gets a little wider. I look around me. The place is now swarming with people in every corner. Anirban has a patient card that he's holding up.

The phone rings. It's my cousin. He wants to know if my dad will help him with a movie script he's writing. OH MY GOD!!! My parents. I'll have to tell them.

Immediately, my brain starts to explode.

How will I tell my parents? Shit. I didn't think about that.

My parents live in Delhi. I am their only child. And I am fiercely protective of my parents. If I had my way, I would shield them from everything bad or sad.

I'm still grappling with that when Anirban tells me we have to go for the MRI. We go down, the three of us. Lost in our thoughts. Wandering through corridors of people. On stretchers, with pipes in their noses, holding IV lines, cutting fruit, waiting, sleeping. A strange world in the innards of the hospital.

After wandering through many doors and passages, each more terrifying than the other, we arrive at the MRI department. There's not even an inch of space to sit or stand. We fight our way to the counter. A number is given, the card is swiped, and we are told this will take a while.

There's no place to sit. And it's already lunchtime. My stomach is rumbling. I'm so used to being an office slave that the minute the clock strikes 1 p.m., my stomach starts to rumble.

We decide to get food.

We step out. And walk away from the hospital, looking for food. I see the same people outside. And I also see the guys selling lanyards. You know, those laminated things that you can slip your office swipe card into. Comes with a ribbon-like thing you drop across your neck.

There are people selling that. My brain tells me, 'There are people selling that kind of thing, for people like you.'

This is where my patient card will go. So now I'll be a file, and a card. My name, what I do, how I feel, the ideas I think of, the brainstorming I do, the clients who listen to me, all that will cease to matter. And I will be a file and card.

Me: Zeebee. It's cancer ☹

We are now hoping it is non-invasive.

I have to have an MRI before they can figure that out.

Am waiting for them to give me a date. Finished registering, etc.

Oinx and Anirban are with me.

Ziba: So fast you got result? Oh gosh Shorms … sorry to hear this. And really sorry I am not there. I will keep checking up with Oinx. U take care of yourself. Lots of hugs. See you soon.

Me: Haha! You can check with me also. I am fine. Will be jumping around.

Ziba: Crack!

Me: Like the doctor said, treat it like a minor irritant. And better call me and treat me normal okay!

Ziba: Done!!!

7

∽

How could I not have seen the signs?

I ignored the lump. In the past, I've always got my lumps checked within weeks of discovering them.

This one, I just watched it grow.

And the nipple going in. Why didn't I just google it? I'm just grateful that I had nothing to do that Saturday afternoon. Or I would have gotten busy with work, or going out to meet friends, or just anything at all, and kept pushing this away. Knowing that something was not right, but just running away from it.

Of course, the flip side is, the fact that I was so careless with this rather obvious sign has imprinted itself on my brain and every other part of my body. Now, I check my solitary nipple like a maniac. Before I sleep, I look to see if it's standing. As soon as I come back from my workout, I peek at it. The sports bra flattens it out and gives me mini heart attacks all the time. But I am obsessed with checking on this nipple. It's sort of a side effect of what happened to me. I kid you not. I have even peeked into my T-shirt while watching TV, just to check if it's all okay. And once I left a meeting, went to the loo, lifted my kurta, and checked. My biggest fear is one day

I'll forget there are other people around and stick my head down the neck of my dress and take a quick look. No, I absolutely do not want people to think I'm some pervy woman who's eyeing her own breasts while out for a meal with friends.

8

s we walked across the road for lunch to a small Udipi place, my mind was scurrying around in circles.

Why did the doctor call it 'the disease'? Why didn't she use the word cancer?

Is it going to kill me? Is it that bad that even the doctor can't get herself to say it?

The boobs she drew? They looked small. Was she judging the size of my boobs?

And they'll need to take out my nipple.

And she asked for an MRI? That's the machine where you go in and suffocate?

Fuccccckkkkkkkk.

The place was packed. Most people looked like patients or families of patients. Again, I saw children, with tubes. Or holding on to a parent's hand. My eyes had already started looking for the files. Was it thick or was it slim? For some reason, my mind was latching on to that. If I saw a thin file, I felt a sense of relief.

We ate dosas and idlis. I don't really remember what we spoke about. I was normal, and talking to Oinx and Anirban, but my mind

51

was still having random conversations with me. And right now, it was telling me that the MRI machine will be the end of me.

I tried hard to eat and keep the food down.

We walked back to the hospital. Oinx asked me if she could tell a friend what the diagnosis was. He knew she was coming with me, and would be worried.

I looked at her. And in that moment of walking back to the hospital, I made the first of many decisions that would influence my journey with cancer.

I told her to please tell him exactly what had happened.

I just knew that's what I will be doing. You know there's no other way to say this. It's like there are a million thoughts in your head, and they are being processed really fast. But even in those tiny milliseconds, you're weighing your decisions, you're watching each one of them, looking at them from every angle, and calmly sifting through those that need to stay and those that don't. Bit like the Harry Potter sorting hat thing. Only it's happening right there, in your head.

Why was this decision a big deal? Because in that instant I decided none of this was my fault. I had nothing to hide. I was not going to blame myself, or keep it a secret. It was cancer. The doctor said it was treatable. So that was it. There was some giant lucky draw that happened in the sky, or rather, some giant not-so-lucky draw, and I got picked. That was it.

Sure, the minute the radiologist told me, I knew. I knew that it was true. Because of the way I had been living, and how all the confusion in my head had spread to my body. I was sure this was a manifestation.

But still, I was not to blame. It was not my fault at all.

In fact, this was a chance to completely change my life, and I was going to grab it with both hands.

And that's why I would tell everyone who wanted to know.

It's pretty funny how all these thoughts keep popping into your head, like some supersonic toaster, just tossing crisp bread out at a manic speed.

Which brings me to a very important point. Why do all hotels, however awesome, fancy, big, pricey they are, never pay attention to the toaster?

They have the most gorgeous breakfast buffets, but the thing toasting your bread is a tiny machine that accepts only two slices at a time, and then those slices fall into a tray and you can't get them out fast enough without burning your fingers, and there's a queue forming behind you, and you want a third toast, but now the person behind you is tapping their fork on the plate.

Dude, hotel people, if you are reading this, please take note. We'd prefer a line of ten toasters to those strange shoe polish machines you have scattered all over your corridors.

But back to my brain popping out thoughts like toast.

Actually, my decision to be open about everything wasn't just based on what I felt in that instant. It came from something that had happened to me about fifteen years back.

I got my first anxiety attack.

Okay, so rewind ... I had just quit my job in advertising, and started writing for television. There was a new channel that had launched, and they were looking to do fresh content that wasn't all saas bahu.

The writing was fun, but working from home was not. This is the first time I was working outside of advertising, and also as a freelance writer. I missed going to office, seeing other people, and having a regulated life. I didn't know how to manage my time. I was worried that I wouldn't have a monthly pay cheque. I wrote all the time to make up for that. I was stressed about writing to impossible deadlines. Yep, I would be writing today, for an episode that was going to be shot tomorrow. Plus, this new world of television was very different from my advertising world. The plots would careen in all directions. I kid you not, one of the shows that I gave up my job to write for, was a coming-of-age show. Like a young adult romance, with this really clumsy, gawky girl in the lead. It was fresh, urban, and pretty cool actually. Then suddenly the channel felt we were being too urban, and this was a general entertainment show, so they turned it into a princess show. Not loosely, but hugely based on *The Princess Diaries*. So of course, the entire plot, everything had to change. And then, get this, they realized that teenagers and young adults weren't their target audience, kids were. So, it became a fantasy adventure.

Like seriously. Enough to give anyone anxiety.

The final blow was, just as I was trying hard to cope with all this, my dog died. She had a heart attack, and died in my arms one evening. I was the only one home, and I had never seen anything or anyone die in front of me. It was devastating. I could hear my heart beating loudly in my ears. I tried calling Anirban to tell him what had happened, and I just couldn't remember how to use the phone. I could just see my dog there, not moving, not breathing, and I found myself gasping for air, trying to keep myself from passing out.

I think I just spiralled into depression from there. I was sad, grieving, lost, floundering.

It started getting worse. I would be lonely. I would skip meals. I would write these shows by day, and watch them in the evening, to see if my writing was working. I would barely leave the house. Some days I would write an emotional scene, and would end up sobbing my eyes out while writing. Or even worse, I would watch it in the evening, and sob again. It's like those characters were the only ones I was hanging out with. And they had very melodramatic lives. It was killing me.

My relationship with my parents was also affected. They came to stay with us for a while. And I fought with them the whole time. They couldn't understand why I was so devastated by my dog dying, and I couldn't understand how they were so insensitive.

They left. And my anxiety grew and grew. Till it reached a point where I started having panic attacks. I would be out, on a familiar street, right next to my house, and suddenly my hands and feet would start going cold. I would feel like I couldn't breathe. My mind and body would start to shut down. And I would feel like I was going to pass out and die.

And remember, this is when no one spoke about anxiety or panic attacks. I hid it for some time, but then it started happening at home. I'd lie in bed and that familiar chill would start on my hands and feet, then the sweating, then the heart racing, then the dry mouth. Ugh. It was the worst.

I thought if I told my husband or my parents, they'd take me to an asylum, and leave me there. Imagine, there was no way to google this. Because this was the initial days of Google and I didn't even know you could google this! I just suffered, and thought I was going mad.

It became so bad that I couldn't do anything. Could not go to a movie hall or a restaurant. Could not go out. Could not meet friends. Could not go into a trial room in a shop. Oh ya, that's because along with the anxiety came claustrophobia, like a faithful sidekick that couldn't just let anxiety do all the work.

It just kept getting bigger. I couldn't watch anything on TV, because it might trigger an attack. I could not read anything apart from *Archie* comics. Which I read like they were a lifeline!

I started to hide what I was feeling even from Anirban. I'd refuse to go out anywhere. I'd beg him not to leave me alone. And when he'd ask what was wrong, I wouldn't tell him.

I didn't even tell my parents. I remember visiting them at some point, while all this was happening. And my mother would take me to meet some friends or neighbours, and I'd tremble. My mouth would feel dry. But I'd go, and it would be agony. Because I was always scared that I'll have an anxiety attack. I think half the anxiety with anxiety attacks is because you're thinking you'll have one any time.

This went on for a long while. Me keeping it inside, hiding it, not letting Anirban help me.

It's hard. You want help. You need help. But you are locked. Plus, in my case I was devastated by what was happening to me. So unprepared and so shocked. I kept thinking I was going mad. And that can be a very scary feeling. I would worry that I'd be put in a mental hospital. That was my biggest nightmare.

Luckily for me, there's some part inside me that's a fighter. That refuses to give up. Or maybe, when you reach rock bottom, there is only one way from there … the internet! Ha, gotcha. But seriously. That's what happened. The internet saved my life. Now this is before Facebook and Gmail and stuff. But this was the times of ASL and chat rooms.

I was part of a community chat room called Thorn Tree that belonged to Lonely Planet. And I would answer questions on India and chat with people from all over. One day, I decided that enough was enough, and I needed help. I asked Anirban to come with me to visit a doctor. I picked a GP I had never visited before. He spent about five minutes listening to me, didn't answer any of my questions, and prescribed some medicines.

The medicines made me groggy as hell. I spent two days barely functioning. Just wandering around the house in my nightclothes, trying hard to stay awake.

I knew the medicines were wrong for me, and so was that doctor. So, in a desperate cry for help, I posted a message on my Thorn Tree group, telling these strangers who I had gotten to know online that I was feeling like I was going mad. I told them about the panic attacks and the anxiety. And the medicines that were not working. And if they had any idea what I could do. And I waited.

It was the right thing to do. Because this group had people from other countries. Who immediately chimed in saying this was a panic attack. And for the first time in months, I realized that I was not alone. If it had a name, and if they knew about it, that meant that it was something that others went through as well.

The oldest member in our little Thorn Tree group was Sterling, an American Buddhist, who was about fifteen years older than me. And Sterling was the one who set the ball rolling. Imagine a girl in Mumbai has anxiety and feels like she's going mad, and a Buddhist American, who she's never met, who is nothing like her, is the one who nudges her on a path that will change so many things.

So that morning, as I'm hunched over my laptop, reading what Sterling has written on the Thorn Tree group, my heart was beating fast. Not out of anxiety this time, but hope. She tells me this is common. And lots of people get help for it, and even get better. All these symptoms were COMMON???? Woohoo, I could dance. She also tells me to try something gentle. Bach flower remedies. Oh, and she asks for the name of the medicine the doctor prescribed and tells me that the medicine is a form of Prozac. I search, and yes it is, and it has all these side effects.

I stop the medicine and start searching online for Bach flower remedies in Mumbai. One pharmacy somewhere in South Mumbai has them. But how was I going to get there? I might have a panic attack just getting there. I continue to search, and I stumble across two Indian doctors, husband and wife, who practise Indian flower remedies. And guess what, their clinic was a short auto ride from home. I filled the form, and I get an appointment for the day after.

I also feel a surge of feel-good hormones. After a long, long time. So, I googled the words 'therapist' and 'Mumbai'. And the first person I found was a Parsi lady who practises cognitive therapy. No medicines, only therapy.

Well, that day was the turning point. I went to the flower remedy doctors. They spoke to me for two hours. They didn't look shocked or puzzled, but they seemed to absolutely understand what I was saying. They gave me some gentle flower remedies. I gathered the courage to go to town, to meet the therapist, and she started working with me, and most importantly, she introduced me to yoga.

The doctors introduced me to clean, organic food. The therapist led me to meditation, working out, and journaling.

And slowly, very, very slowly, I started getting better. Imagine, you are lying on your bed and suddenly you get hit by a panic attack and you feel you'll fall out of the window. It's that bad. And then slowly, months and months later … that feeling goes. You can now lie on the bed without being afraid of being swallowed up by it.

Sterling came to India and stayed with us for a month. I learnt so much from her. Surya namaskars. How beautiful the goddess Tara is. And also, she said something that has helped me so many times. I was sitting with her by the window and telling her how much I've changed. How confident, how fearless I used to be. And now I have all these anxieties and some claustrophobia and everything else. And she said, 'Don't dwell over what you were, think about what you will be from here.'

I think that line has just stayed with me. The funny part is, I didn't know it'll come in use again, so many years later.

Anyway, my anxiety eased off. Some stuff took months, some took years. Like flying. I just couldn't fly for years. The claustrophobia or the fear of having an anxiety attack in a closed place was so bad. It was also triggered by the fact that I got my first panic attack in an aircraft.

It took me six years to start flying again. I'd just go everywhere by train. Which was a bummer, and took too much time, and it also meant dragging friends, family, and colleagues by train and having them crib. It also meant missing out on holidays, workshops abroad, shoots. But there was no option. I took it slow and tried to just let it take its own time.

My biggest learning from my anxiety attacks was the advice that Sterling gave me. And the second was something Anirban told me. The anxiety almost ripped us apart. It was very, very hard on our relationship. I would be so secretive and uncommunicative, and didn't even want to tell those who loved me what was wrong with me. And one day, the therapist asked if we'd like to do a joint session. So, we did. And Anirban said something to me. He said that I shut him out. I tried to do this on my own. There was no space for anyone to help me.

This time around, I wasn't going to make that mistake. I couldn't make that mistake. I just knew he would be my pillar. And that I would let him be that. And I also knew that I wouldn't try and do this on my own. I would ask anyone and everyone for help. I would take my friends, my family, people who loved me, people who knew me, and even those who didn't, with me.

I would talk. I would reach out. I would not do any of this alone.

And that was one of the best decisions I took.

9

We walk back to the hospital, and take the stairs down to the innards. We cross over, go to the next wing, and enter the area for the MRI.

If anything, there are more people here. We wade through them all. I go back into being in a daze. I see, but I don't see. The kid in a hospital bed, in the corridor, hooked up to tubes. Rows of people, sad faces, hopeless faces, talking slowly, in hushed tones. Everyone looks like they've been waiting forever.

We make our way to the MRI section. It's closed off. Only the patient is allowed inside. I start to feel a little ball of panic in the pit of my stomach.

Will I have to go in there alone?

What if my claustrophobia kicks in?

Will they be able to stop it and pull me out in time before I have an anxiety attack?

I haven't had an anxiety attack in ages. But who can say.

I start remembering all the horror stories. A colleague, big, strapping man, who had to have an MRI. He said when he went into that doughnut-shaped machine and realized he was strapped in and it just kept closing in on him, he went absolutely ballistic. He said that they took what he felt was a long time to get him out.

He didn't complete the MRI.

And then I remembered a newspaper article. Where a ward boy had walked into an MRI chamber with an oxygen cylinder, and he got stuck to the machine. And by the time they managed to get him out, his organs were damaged. The magnetic force was that much.

Fuccccccckkkkk. I have braces.

Alarm bells start ringing in my head.

Okay, now before you ask why a forty-four-year-old has braces, this is my jinx. I have had braces for ten years. On and off. The first time they were awesome. My teeth looked like a white bhutta. So perfect and pretty. However, to put braces, they first have to remove two teeth on the top and two on the bottom. When everything gets pushed back, and the teeth get aligned, the gaps go away.

Except in my case, the gaps didn't go away because we removed the braces too soon. Actually, I begged and pleaded with the orthodontist to remove them. He wasn't happy, but he did it. And for the first few years, they were bhutta quality. Then the gaps started coming back again, till finally I had two gaping bits on both sides. I hated it.

I went to another dentist. Big mistake. This one was taking so much time over my teeth that I was beginning to suspect he was building the Taj Mahal in my mouth. I'd go to him, and he'd tinker with the braces for five minutes and then chat with me for twenty. And in my head, I'd be asking him all sorts of questions. Like, are you really doing anything at all? Why do these braces never feel like they've been tightened? Why have the gaps not reduced even by a millimetre? And will you please stop talking to me and get my teeth fixed!

But instead, I'd smile most enthusiastically and chat with him about his holiday plans and tell him mine.

I think for some reason, he thought I had a very interesting life. So, I'd feel compelled to feed that fantasy. And I'd start blabbering about a shoot we did, or a film we made. It was a big mistake, because two years later, the gaps were still firmly in place.

So now, I was standing there, right outside the MRI area, freaking out, thinking my mouth could get glued to the machine.

The MRI area was a massive basement parking kind of waiting room. There was a door on one side which led to where the doctors and machines were. The door was guarded by a couple of hospital staff. And I didn't blame them. Remember how all hell broke loose as soon as the gyneac arrived, and how everyone ran and stood outside her door and every time an assistant opened it, at least three people tried to push themselves in?

This is how we are. We'll wait patiently for hours. At the bus stop, doctor's chamber, or even the aircraft. Then as the bus arrives, boom, the line is gone … everyone is trying to get through that narrow door first. You know the aircraft landing drill.

But then, it's in my genes as well. I begged Anirban to push his way in and ask the doctor if they'll do my MRI with the braces. No point waiting here for ages if they said no. I think some part of me was wanting to run away. Okay, maybe every part of me was hoping to run away.

Just then an assistant opened the door and called us in. We took off our shoes and walked into a very brightly lit corridor. Anirban went to show the ward assistant my file, and I looked around. There were rooms on either side. And one room on the right had a large glass sliding door. It has radiation symbols drawn all around it. Plus, it had a huge red light over it, and what looked like a giant buzzer on the side. It was what they used to open the door.

I was shit scared. But there was no option.

The great thing about having Anirban with me was he just handled everything. I was like a rather slow zombie who was grinning and talking, but who was incapable of being efficient and organized. I needed someone to do things for me, and he just took over that role.

Anirban came back saying we had to do a blood test and they can't do the MRI without it. So off we went again, into this labyrinth of a hospital. I felt like a prisoner on parole.

After asking around, we were directed to the place where they did blood tests. And my heart sank. It was a massive room, like a basement, low ceilings, dimly lit, filled with people. Sick, and frail. Gloom hung over that room. This day was like no other. I wanted to cry. I felt hopeless, like my number would never come. How could one hospital ever treat so many people?

We made our way to the reception desk. It was crowded. We waited, waved our papers, stood in line, and finally it was our turn. The lady at the counter took our card, then she looked at Anirban and said, 'If you can afford private, please go upstairs and get your blood test done.'

This was the general ward.

We turned and left. My heart was so sad, and yet I breathed a huge sigh of relief. For where I was born, for the fact that I could afford private. Never have I been more aware of my privilege than in that hospital.

In fact, I have an idea. All offenders, big or small, traffic or murder, must spend a proportionate time working at the Tata Memorial general ward. There can be no greater lesson than having to see that level of suffering every day.

Upstairs, the sun had come out. The giant hall had far less people. We reached the place where you took a token for the blood test, and they said they would close at 3 p.m. We had twenty minutes. If our number came, then great. Or else we'd have to come back.

We sat in the waiting area, our eyes on the board that flashed token numbers. Suddenly I wanted this over today. Now that I knew what it was, I wanted to know what the next steps were. And the thought of coming back again to this place, and the MRI, I just wanted it over.

Token numbers kept flashing. It was going to be touch and go.

The board changed, and it was my number. I was the last person to get a blood test that day.

They told us they'll give the report in forty-five minutes. I used the time to call my dentist. I tried to keep it as casual and normal as possible.

Hi Doctor, this is Shormistha. How are you? Doctor, sorry I'm calling on your mobile, but it's urgent. I've just been diagnosed with breast cancer, and they want to do an MRI. What metal are my braces made of? And you think I'll be able to do an MRI with them?

He's shocked. Says he's so sorry to hear this. And am I okay?

And I tell him I'm absolutely fine. And that sort of sets the pattern for how I'll break the news to everyone.

I realize just listening to his tone, that everyone is going to be shocked, sad, and everything in between. If I keep calm, and just stick to the facts and laugh and say hey, I'm fine, then they'll be fine. It's going to be my bedside manner for the next week or two.

Only I didn't realize how much of the bedside manner I will be required to use!

The good news was my braces are made of stainless steel. They will not impact the MRI, and I am not likely to have my mouth glued to the machine. Hurrah!

The report arrives, and off we go to the MRI room. Anirban goes in to give them the file, and we wait. It's been a long day. We've been in the hospital since 8.45 a.m., I've been told I have breast cancer, and this day is still not ending.

Finally, I am called in again. Only one person can come into the waiting area with me. Oinx waits outside, while Anirban comes with me. The assistant looks at all my reports, and then hands the file to another assistant. We're sitting on a bench waiting. I'm just staring at THAT room. Someone is inside, because the big red light is on. The assistants and doctors are walking around, doing their thing. And I'm thinking how it's just a normal day for everyone. How everyone I know is going about stuff, my colleagues, my friends, my family. And I find myself wishing it was a normal day for me.

Suddenly the assistant comes back. There's a particular medicine that has to be bought. A medicine they will inject me with, and it has to be purchased and replaced by the patient.

Everything happened so fast. I just realized while writing this, that I never even asked what the blood test was for. In my head, I consider that time as BC (Before Cancer). When I was an innocent newbie. Little did I know that I'll have medical terms coming out of my ears soon.

Anyway, the medicine is a dye they'll inject me with. Wow, I can see it coursing through my veins, turning everything blue or green. I want to ask the ward assistant more questions but he has no time. He hands Anirban the name of the medicine and then tells me to take off all my earrings and nose rings. I tell him I have braces. He says he'll have to check with the doctor. Anirban is leaving, he sends Oinx in, in his place. I'm starting to panic just a little. Things are suddenly moving too fast.

I tug all the earrings out. But I don't want to remove my nose stud and nose ring. I have no idea why. Possibly because I don't know when I'll ever be able to put them back on. Second, because I have never taken them out. I don't know how to.

I plead with the assistant. He says he'll check with the doctor, but I need to get changed fast. He points me in the direction of a room. It's like a storage room, plus a blood-test room, plus a changing room. On one side is a bunch of hospital pyjamas and tops. I pick up a set. But there's no place to change or shut the door. You basically have to duck behind the door, so no one in the corridor can see you, and quickly wiggle your way out of your clothes and into those.

I duck and do the whole thing as fast as I can, and as I straighten up, I hit my head on the door handle really hard. My head spins. And I'm thinking wow, first cancer and now brain damage.

I stagger out holding my head. And Oinx is looking hassled. They want me in, now. But where is Anirban? How can I go in without seeing him first? I'm starting to panic.

This is a busy hospital. And there are hundreds of patients waiting. The attendants are telling me to get ready to go in. What if I feel like peeing in the middle of it? I ask the assistant how long it'll take and he says forty-five minutes.

He also tells the nurse to tape up my nose rings. And they're opening the big glass door for me. Last minute, I lose my nerve. And I ask them if someone can come in with me. I'm expecting them to laugh and say no.

But surprisingly, they say yes. Oinx immediately stands up and says she'll come. I look at her. This girl has severe claustrophobia. She can't even get a facial treatment done, because it freaks her out to close her eyes with all that goop on her face and eyelids. And she's coming into a sealed room with me?

Instantly I feel better. I feel like we'll both see each other through.

We walk into the room. There's a massive glass panel on one side. Behind it sit the technicians and the doctors. I can see them talking, walking, going about their life. In the middle of the room is this big machine. With a circle in the centre that I will slide into. On one side is an open cupboard filled with a jumble of blankets and sheets. There's an attendant lady and man who follow us in. They point to the chair in the corner that Oinx will need to sit on. And they ask me to open my shirt, lie on my stomach on the sliding part of the machine, and place my breasts in what looks like an egg tray. And then they'll put a blanket on me, so I don't freeze with my bum up. And oh, if flashing my boobs at the attendant and all the people behind the screen isn't enough, I also have to be wearing huge ass headphones. Because when the machine starts, there will be massive noise.

I bare my boobs, and they adjust the tray, and it's a strange way to be. I'm looking at the blanket which they are going to put on me. It reminds me of the Rajdhani blankets. Brown, and not the cleanest. But I shut out these thoughts, and I grin, and I ask Oinx if she's okay. She's also wearing headphones. I see big eyes looking back at me. And I am filled with so much gratitude and love. That she's walked into this claustrophobic room that will be locked up, only to support me.

I gather strength from that. To know that I am loved.

I have to stop here to talk about something. My idea of dealing with unpleasant things is to quickly get it over with. It's like eating karela before you tackle all the tasty stuff on your plate. That day, to bare your breasts to random strangers, who are laughing and chatting behind a screen, it didn't make any difference. I remember a time I got terrible food poisoning, and had to be rushed to hospital in the middle of the night. While barfing and just about keeping my knees from buckling under me as Anirban bundled me into an auto, one thought kept flashing in my head: *You are not wearing a bra. And your sleeping T-shirt is so worn out, it has holes.* My brain was screeching this shit like those ladies in the Mumbai locals who make big eyes and nod at your bra straps if they stick out of your clothes.

But my body eventually overpowers the brain. And it was like, *dude, you worry too much. Here puke once more, no time to think.*

But this was different. And especially if you are shy or conscious, or don't know how to deal with this. The trauma of it all. I understand that the healthcare system is burdened, but not to show any empathy is truly sad. Why can't they have women attendants? And a screen where you can't see all the chatting, grinning technicians and doctors.

It would make something so traumatic just a little easier, for all the women who come there.

Anyway, back to me. I'm lying stomach down on a sliding bed. I'm tied down by straps. The front of my gown is open, and my boobs are in a tray. And I have giant headphones on. I was so scared till a while ago. I'm still scared, but now also so amused at how on a regular working day, I ended up looking like a topless DJ about to enter a doughnut.

The attendants clear off. I tell myself to stay calm. Oinx is smiling at me. The doors are sealed. And the red light comes on. They tell me not to move. Like really! And then it starts. I start sliding into that hole. And they are giving me all sorts of instructions. I'm keeping my entire being focused on that, because I don't want to be freaking out. And that's when the sound starts. A crazy loud sound, like they are drilling the walls and the floor. I can hear it through the headphones. And by Oinx's expression, so can she.

I slide into the doughnut. The walls are inches away from me. But I am not freaking out, no claustrophobia. I am okay. My body starts to relax. I know I'll get through whatever there is in store for me. If I can do this, then I can do the rest.

They keep sliding me in and out. The noise stops. I tell Oinx, 'Damn, they could have picked a better soundtrack.' Oinx is grinning and saying, 'Should we ask them for the playlist?'

'Please don't move and talk.' The doctors are not amused.

After that, another twenty minutes of sliding around, of having that crazy noise fill the room, and we are done. The red light goes off. The tube lights come on. The door opens. I wait. I swear if I hadn't been strapped to the bed, I would have leapt and run out of the place, probably flashing everyone on the way. I wonder if that's why they tie people up?

They remove the straps, take away the tray, and ask me to gently haul myself up. It's done. My nemesis, my arch enemy, my nightmare. I want to dance.

And then it strikes me this is only the beginning.

We leave the hospital. It's been a long day. We pile into Oinx's car, and head back home. I'm just happy to get away from the hospital. It's still gloomy, and Parel with its monorail flyover looks even more cramped and Dickensian.

I feel it in my bones that the MRI will confirm the cancer. I don't want to deal with it today.

I suddenly remember that I was supposed to meet a friend's parents in the evening. I call them and of course they want to know how I am. So, I tell them, that the doctor said it is cancer, but we're waiting for the MRI to confirm it. The doctor also said it's nothing to worry about. And I feel fine.

And then because they are warm, easy-going people, I tell them to join me for an evening of drinking and dinner. Most importantly, I know they will not freak out, and we'll all have a good chat and a laugh.

So that evening, I stand outside one of the nicest neighbourhoods in my area. And laugh and ask for a smoke.

I take two puffs. I drink some wine. And I eat a great meal.

Very dramatic.

But hey, I just got told that I have 'the disease'.

I'm allowed some drama, and some denial, right?

10

I had a weekend to make the most of my life. Friday was the MRI, results were expected Monday. Nicely timed by the cancer gods.

So, I decided to live it up, in between bouts of trying to wrap my head around the practicalities.

First was telling people. Divided into two kinds. The ones I loved. And the ones that would need to be told.

Topping that list were my folks.

Now why is there no ready reckoner on how to tell your parents that you have cancer?

Anirban and I spent most of Saturday trying to figure out if we should tell my parents now or later. And then we decided to tell them as early in the journey as possible. So they had time to process everything.

Anirban's parents lived in the flat above us. We decided not to tell them. They were older, and his mom had heart issues and blood pressure, and it just wasn't worth telling them till we knew how bad it was, and what we had to do.

Next was telling Anirban's sister, Koeli didi. And a friend, Himanshu, who had a bout with cancer and came out of it. I figured he'd be great to talk to.

Also, by now the news had spread. Most of my closest friends knew. Lot of my colleagues knew. People were beginning to call. And give advice.

Let's talk about that for a bit.

First here's a short 101 on how to react when someone tells you they have cancer. Or more importantly, how not to react.

'Oh my god, never, no, I am freaking out.'

Not a good way to react. If you are telling me that you are freaking out, then I should be exploding with stress. Like really, what's the logic? You are not going to go through the treatment or the chemo, or have your boob taken out, so you have no reason to freak out.

'No, it can't be, I don't believe this.'

Uh, you better. Unless you are an oncologist who knows more than the one I met. I know that you mean that it's hard and you don't want this to happen to me, but you can't keep repeating *I don't believe this* because it makes me want to cry, and say I can't believe it either.

'Why is this happening to you? You are such a good person.'

Honestly, this was the most irritating response. How the fuck do I know why it's happening to me? And why are you linking some hormonal or cellular (not the mobile network obviously) glitch in my system to me being good or bad? What about kids who get cancer? Are they good people or bad people? And this entire sentence somehow makes me feel like a fraud. Like if I was REALLY a good person this would never have happened. Also, just so you know, Mother Teresa died of a heart attack. There is no rule that says good people die peacefully in their sleep, clutching a photo of their favourite dog, and a smile playing on their lips.

One second, now I'm comparing myself to dead people?? All because of you!

'But you are so healthy. You do yoga and you cycle and you eat right.'

Really? You ignorant fool! Remember, Lance Armstrong had cancer. And this man cycled all the time. Oh, you probably wore a Livestrong band because you thought it was a fashion accessory. And wait a minute, what about Yuvi? That strapping Punjab da munda cricketer. What connection does yoga, or cycling, or being fit have with cancer? Have you been researching medical statistics in your spare time, that it surprises you that healthy people can get cancer? Ugh. So bloody stupid.

No, I'd say none of this to the folks who reacted with these statements. And believe me, a majority of people reacted with at least one or a variation of these.

This is what I would have liked to tell them, but I was in a daze. I was going through everything feeling very calm, and Mother Teresa-like. I'd tell a person, watch their reaction, and then in my best bedside manner reassure them that I was fine. That it would be okay, I would get through it. Apart from patting their head and taking their hand in mine, I was doing everything else.

It was funny. All these people going to pieces, and the patient going, 'There, there.'

After the reaction came the advice. I swear, it's like most folks had a hack or a doctorate on cancer.

The most common advice was to ask me to drop my doctor, and go see a doctor they had heard of. When I'd say no, they'd say, 'But you are getting a second opinion, right?'

I don't get it. What is with this doctor shopping? I go to an onco with shitloads of experience in the country's biggest cancer hospital, and I like her. So why a second opinion? Is this like wholesale sari shopping in Chandni Chowk, that I should go from doctor to doctor? And how will I know which one is giving me correct advice? No, thanks. I would rather listen to my gut and go with this lady. Plus, she was my age. I felt like she wouldn't bullshit or patronize me.

The second advice was to see an Ayurvedic doctor. Almost everyone seemed to have one. Just like everyone seems to have a favourite restaurant where the staff knows them, and the chef comes and says hi, and then they order off the menu. I, of course, have none of that, except the fruitwala whose eyes light up when he sees me. Because he knows I'm a bleeding heart who never bargains. And he plays a game called, 'How much can I overcharge her for one pomegranate?' I'm always the loser in this game.

Ya, so I felt very left out, and made a mental note to get myself an Ayurvedic doctor when this was over.

And of course, there were some well-meaning folks, who insisted I should go see an Ayurvedic doctor, tarot card reader, healer, and even a leaf doctor that weekend itself. Okay, so I'm not dissing these people. I have a lot of faith in alternate healing. But I just got to know on Friday that I have cancer, and on Saturday/Sunday you want me to rush around meeting all these people.

I have a lot of things to do.

Like attending the Swan Lake ballet and a friend's birthday bash at a bar.

You could say I was in denial. And now, in retrospect, I'd probably buy that.

But I also think that my sense of optimism had kicked in. And secretly in my head, I was convinced that this was going to be cancer lite. Fine, there'll be a surgery and then that's it. It'll be over, and I'll have the chance to start my life afresh. So naive.

Here's the strange thing. A friend who knew a cancer survivor insisted I get in touch with her. I was reluctant. This weekend I just wanted to live my regular life. In fact, I went cycling both days. I didn't want any more advice. But finally, after much persuasion, I dropped this person a message.

And I remember she called just as Oinx and I were on our way to see the Russians perform Swan Lake. I've never been to the ballet, and I was super excited. Also, because I love the chicken sandwiches and cold coffee at the National Centre for the Performing Arts. And if there was anything that could cheer me up, it was that.

So, she called and asked how I am. And the call happened when Oinx and I were driving down the Sea Link bridge, listening to music, feeling happy, and I laughed and said I'd been diagnosed with breast cancer. And she paused and said, 'How are you feeling?' I replied in my most chirpy voice, 'Totally fine. Not stressed. I'll just take it as it comes.' And she said, 'Oh, you're in denial.'

Something inside me froze. I didn't like her. I quickly ended the conversation. It troubled me. I expected her to say, 'You have this, sister.' Not to say I was in denial.

But I was. Now when I look back, it was a coping mechanism. I was refusing to believe that it would be bad. I just wanted to go out, go to work, cycle, loaf around, and live my life. Hoping the cancer would not be able to catch up.

What that conversation also taught me was that people were not always going to react the way I wanted them to. That it would be hard for them. Some because they loved me. Some because it was a shock. And some because they would bring their own experiences into it.

Actually, the funniest reaction was from a close friend of mine. I remember I was just leaving home to go to the hospital for a biopsy when she called. And I figured she had heard about my diagnosis by now. I picked up the call and I was like hey. And she said hello, how are you?

And I of course jumped the gun, and said, 'I'm fine. Don't worry about me. On my way to the hospital. But the spirit is up, koi tension nahi hain.'

She was quiet.

Then I paused. 'You know, na? That I've been diagnosed with breast cancer?'

And she mumbled something, 'Achcha, okay. We'll talk. I have to go now. Okay?'

I was like okay!

And then I realized that's another kind of reaction. Where you don't know what to say. When you are floundering.

Like when a friend's husband died. And I just could not get myself to go to see her. What could I say that would make it okay?

Finally, I mustered up the courage to see her. When I told her how hard it was for me, and how I didn't know what to say, she said something I'll never forget. She said, 'Even if you come and say nothing, it's okay. Just by coming to see me, you make me feel better.'

And that's how it is with cancer. Either people are saying the wrong things, or they're not making eye contact with you, or they are rushing to get off the phone because they are so freaked out.

But the simplest thing to do is to say, 'You'll get through this.' Or, 'I'm thinking about you and sending you so much love and hugs.' Or even the most banal, 'You're a strong girl, and you'll get through this.'

The weekend whooshed by. I went out both nights. I also wore my nicest clothes. The doctor had told me they might have to remove a breast. Or at least a part of it. From her tone, I just had this feeling that they would go all the way. Especially because the lump was so near my nipple.

That was it then. I was going to air my boobs. While I had both of them. So, I wore my most cleavage-popping clothes that weekend, and felt very happy. My boob would go down with a last hurrah.

What was also running through my mind was my relationship with my boobs. When I was a teenager, my mom took me to buy my first bra during summer holidays at my grandparents.

We went to a typical hosiery shop, where Uncle sizes up your chest with his eyes, and then yells to a bored guy, 'Beta, Liberty 30B dena.' Beta climbs up a ladder into a loft and chucks down packets of bras yelling the sizes at the top of his voice as they come hurtling down. This is all absolutely normal and no one bats an eyelid. Except you are so embarrassed that you just want to run out of the shop, forsaking the cold drink that has been offered to you and your mom. The shop guys know this is your first bra and it'll take time.

This shop is pretty radical. They have a woman behind the counter. The bras arrive in cardboard boxes. With pictures of women wearing torpedo-shaped bras. Colours, underwire, padding, sorry, none of that. These have thick straps and are white. Because young girls only got white bras back then. To have a black bra, you'd need to be pretty wild!

I'm standing behind Mom, she's the one taking a call which brand it will be. Not that there is much to choose from. Finally, I am handed two bras and told to try them on. I do that and of course, Mom comes to take a final look. The shop girl also peeks in to see. Yep, that's how it used to be back then. Privacy was the name of a white girl, and not a concept that anyone in India ever understood. Least of all your parents and shop attendants.

They look at me. The cup size is fine, but the shoulder straps are tight. The woman attendant turns to Mom and says, 'Broad shoulders hain na?'

Just four innocuous words. But words that obviously land deep inside me and come up much later.

I have broad shoulders?

Aren't boys supposed to have broad shoulders?

No, this is not good.

I sailed through life with absolutely no body issues. Now that I think of it, it's probably because I was just not aware or conscious of my body. I just took it for granted, and wore the clothes I liked. I never even worked out till I was in my mid-thirties.

All that mattered to me was that I looked okay, and I was happy. I had no time to be critical about anything. In fact, I had buck teeth for a large part of my life, and I was absolutely okay with it. I have a strange, high-pitched voice, but I don't even notice that. It's only when others tell me that, that I'm like, wait a minute, really? But none of it ever stayed in my head or bothered me.

Then as I hit my forties, it started to surface. Do I have broad shoulders? Wait a minute, do I have small boobs? I don't know if it was midlife crisis, or the fact that I looked fabulous in my thirties.

At least in my head.

See, these things are very tricky. A well-meaning person once wrote to me, complimenting me on my blog and the stuff I wrote, and she said, 'Thank you for helping me with my body issues'. And I was like, 'What? How?' And the person told me that she hated her feet and thought they looked ugly. And then she saw I had put up a picture of my feet on my blog, and felt like if I could show my feet and not be conscious, then so could she.

Of course, I thanked her. And said great going.

But it bothered me. I thought my feet were great looking. So why did she think if I can put up mine … wait … did she think my feet are ugly? Are my feet ugly? What the fuck, I have ugly feet!

I sailed through life thinking I look awesome, but maybe that's only in my own head.

So ya, that's how these things come back. Like the broad shoulders suddenly pops back in my head, from the cold storage it festered in all these years. And in my forties, I'm convinced that I have small boobs, and that's why my shoulders look big. I make fun of my boobs all the time. Calling them lemons and raisins, and cribbing to my girlfriends that I want plastic surgery.

Also, I have a big ass. Which I hated when I was growing up. Till Jennifer Lopez came along. And then I was like, 'Wait a minute, my ass is in fashion? Okay then, let's not hide it under long shirts anymore.'

But my boobs, nope, small boobs never really became fashionable. Of course, they meant I could wear racerbacks, and halter necks and everything else, but still, the joke stayed. And I always laughed and made fun of my boobs.

Well, guess what, not being happy with my boobs and making fun of them, it just bit me on my ample ass.

Also, maybe there's a lesson there somewhere.

Be happy with what you have.

And don't listen to shop attendants.

Imagine, all these thoughts happening over forty-eight hours.

What madness.

And to top it all, on Sunday we decided to tell my mom and dad that their only child has been diagnosed with breast cancer.

11

You never call us on FaceTime. But you did that day. I took the call and you said where is Poppy, I want to talk to him also. I want to talk to both of you.

Little did I know what you were going to say to us.

I thought, all right, great, today what's happened to her. What change has come over her, that she's calling on FaceTime?

Nobody would have ever prepared me for what was coming.

Anyway, we sat down, because you said, 'I have something to tell you.'

And this is what you told us. That you've been to Tata Memorial and they've checked that you have this lump, and you had it for a while, and they confirmed … it was the C word.

And you said we still don't know what'll happen next, but I wanted you guys to know.

And I heard you, and now I think maybe I put on a big act. I think my best acting skills, I put to use that day.

And I said, 'Okay, don't worry.' Or something to that effect.

I kept saying, 'All right, it's okay, doesn't matter, tell me what happened, all the details.' And then I said it'll all get sorted out, we are with you. And you go to the doctor and let's see.

You were brave. You didn't say come with me to the doctor. You went with Anirban and a friend. And if you took it on the chin, I had no business to be on FaceTime and crying in front of you.

And that was it.

And afterwards we both cried and cried. Your father and me.

—Mom

12

ᗯ

It was hard telling Mom and Dad. Because I felt like I was letting them down.

I was their only daughter and my job was to protect them from any kind of pain or hurt. And I was going to cause them unimaginable grief.

I felt guilty for doing this. For getting cancer. And I wasn't even going to be there, to hold them.

I knew they'd cry. I knew they'd be miserable miles away from me. I wondered if they'd be able to sleep at night.

If they'd hold each other. If they'd go grey with shock. If they'd fall sick.

My heart was breaking.

I called my cousin, who lives in Gurgaon. And I told him the news. He took it really well. And I told him to call them, and go and see them. And just be with them for a while. And of course, after I called them, I howled my head off.

In retrospect, I don't know why I felt guilty. I didn't feel guilty about anything. I accepted my diagnosis with a lot of peace. Then what caused this feeling?

It's complicated, as Facebook so glibly puts it.

13
ᗯ

M onday arrived.
And I was most definitely going to the office. No way was
I going to sit in dread at home.

I had already mailed everyone on Sunday night.

To: TeamFlyingCursor
From: Shormistha

Subject: I got news for you

Hi everyone,

*So I thought I'd drop an email before there's any speculation, or before
you guys start wondering what's up with me.*

*I've been away from the office last week because I had some medical
concerns.*

Turns out I have breast cancer.

Now here's the thing, I am not dying!

I am going to be absolutely okay. On Monday or Tuesday I'll know the extent of it, and then they'll do some more tests, and then there will be surgery and treatment.

I don't know how long it will take.

But I have been told that I should lead a regular life. Cycle, swim, yoga, kathak, and work!!!

This cancer is really common now, and loads of people work their way through it.

So that is that. You guys are not just my colleagues, you are family. Considering I spend more time with you guys than my family! Which is why I wanted you guys to know.

I'll be in and out of the office for a while as this thing unfolds. And I know while I focus on getting better, that's going to put an extra burden on some of you.

So help each other, partner across departments, and seniority, look at the details, dig deeper when, you work and do great work as usual.

And I'll fight a good fight till then :)

Cheers!

It was all going to be okay. Except, it was strange. Everyone was nice to me, like super nice. Maybe too nice. People were asking me if I wanted to order anything for lunch. Someone had got prawns for me. And in general, I felt like lots of eyes were watching me over their laptops.

Plus, I wasn't really there. Who cared about which idea was better and which client was calling for a meeting? All I wanted to do was run to the loo, and touch the lump and see if it was growing bigger by the minute.

Finally, I gave up the pretence, sat on my desk, and decided to google the damn thing. And boy, what a scary, dark place Doctor Google is.

In about fifteen minutes, I was convinced I was going to die. I had tears in my eyes, and I sat there hoping no one would notice me as I frantically blinked them back.

My phone pinged. It was Anirban. The results were out. The MRI confirmed the cancer.

Nah, I didn't go to pieces. I already knew it. The doctors had done the test to confirm it, even though they seemed sure. But now there was a whole bunch of other tests to do.

Starting with the biopsy.

Next morning, we were back at Tata Memorial. The doctors were having an incredibly busy day. And a junior doctor comes to talk to us. She looks at the MRI report which Anirban has taken printouts of. And then tells us to get an appointment for a biopsy. But she also tells us that there is a big research conference happening and everyone is going to be super busy attending that, so it might take a while. There's also a bunch of blood tests that need to be done.

We go back into the belly of the hospital, wade through the crowds, and get an appointment for ten days later.

I feel sick in my stomach. Ten whole days of just living like this. Suspended in a twilight zone, without Robert Pattinson to come and bite me. Plus, I'm so scared of this hospital. I am ashamed to say this, but I could imagine myself lying in some dreary corridor on a bed, waiting for someone to come attend to me.

The doctor has told me that for the paying public, a private ward exists, but by now the fact that I first heard the news of my diagnoses here and also the crowds, the cloudy days, everything was filling me with hopelessness. And I don't want to be here.

I remember Tarini's offer.

Tarini is a friend and colleague. Possibly my most connected friend, thanks to her family and of course growing up in Delhi. She gets teased massively for this. And considering some of us have been upgraded when travelling with her, and also had airport staff escort us in like celebrities, she's probably our only ticket to lifestyles of the rich and the famous.

She's also a darling. And someone who is like family to me. Plus, she has all the control freak instincts that I do. So, when I told her about my diagnosis, she told me that years back, someone close to her had a brush with cancer. And he went to this doctor, who is immensely trusted by the family, and would I also like to get in touch?

And while I'm not big on doctor shopping expeditions, I am lost. What do I do now? Keep waiting? Find another doctor?

So, I ping Tarini. Who in the meantime has got trays filled with soil installed in her window. (Yes, we live in Mumbai. We install everything in our windows, from gardens, to cylinders, to sports equipment, to even our pets sometimes.)

Anyway, she's started growing a mini farm of wheatgrass for me. Apparently, wheatgrass is really good for cancer.

Ha! At this stage, I'm so freaking out with the delay, that I'll get down on all fours and graze on all the wheatgrass in the world.

I ping her asking if she could connect me to her doctor. Anirban in the meantime has a brainwave. He remembers the oncologist at Tata Memorial, the one I liked and scared with my enthu-ness, telling us that if we have insurance and are covered, then we could also consider going to a private hospital. And she would recommend her teacher who was the head of the breast cancer department at Kokilaben Dhirubhai Ambani Hospital.

We message her asking for his name. And then call Kokilaben Hospital. I'm in luck because I get an appointment for the next day. Which is super rare. Because with time I realize that the cancer department is a cross between the Kumbh Mela and a local train. It is so crowded that chairs in the waiting area are a premium. The minute someone gets called in by a doctor, at least four people rush to grab their seat. I have considered taking my folding chair and going there.

My parents on the other hand have also spoken to a doctor, who is very close to them. He's asked for my report. They've also gone and spoken to many other people. At that moment, I had no headspace to ask them who all they were talking to. But now Mom tells me that Dad has called a lot of people. I think he took it very hard. Mom is stronger, or pretends to be stronger way better. Dad, who was a fighter pilot, fought a war, got shot, got a bullet through his knee, managed to make it back, and continued to fly like a pro, is terrified of hospitals and needles. I kid you not. You know how people go hysterical and freak out at the sight of cockroaches, my dad is like that with injections.

And talking to people was only making it worse.

Actually, that's where it started. We were so clueless, and also in different cities. They had no way to see that I looked absolutely normal and felt normal also. They kept thinking that I'm hiding all my fear and pain from them. And then of course there were people, well-meaning people, who recounted their experiences to them. The only problem is, it kept making it worse. With the stories they heard, their dread for the surgery, and eventually the chemo, kept building.

I, in the meantime, was just hoping Kokilaben Hospital and the new doctor would turn out okay.

That evening, I went to the hospital close to my house to get some blood tests done, which had been prescribed by the junior doctor at Tata Memorial. I still didn't know which doctor, and which hospital, I would end up at, so I was carrying on as usual. Or rather, as usual as could be.

The next day, Anirban takes a half-day off from work. I'm already beginning to feel bad about the number of days he's having to take off. And yes, this is not even counting how I just dropped out of work one fine day. I know it's going to be tough on my partners, my business heads, creative heads, and everyone.

My appointment is for 3 p.m. I wore the same clothes that I wore to Tata Memorial, and we set off.

Kokilaben Hospital is the opposite of Tata Memorial. It's crowded as hell. But if Tata Memorial is all socialist, then this is the McDonald's of capitalism. The air conditioning is on full blast, the lobby is filled with plush sofas, and it's got shops on the ground floor. I spy a salon, a bookstore, a sunglasses stall, and a Starbucks. This could be a shopping mall, where you make a detour for cancer!

Okay now here's a question. Who is coming here to buy sunglasses? Okay, forget that. Who is coming here with a sick person and saying, 'Hey, one minute, while they draw blood from you or even cut you up in the OT, let me just try out that lovely Wayfarer.'

Or are the patients going 'Hurrah, you just fixed my appendix, that calls for a new set of Ray-Bans.'

I really can't wrap my head around that counter. But seeing the salon, the Starbucks, the big medical store filled with comforting odds and ends, I immediately start to cheer up. Not that I'm going to be browsing or getting pedicures, which as you know I owe a great deal to. But still.

We go to the reception counter, register, and make our way to the cancer department. Bright lights, floor stickers that tell you where to go, water dispensers, and wait ... even a Café Coffee Day. That's two coffee shops in one hospital. I don't know why I am so excited, I barely even drink coffee.

But there is a part of me that's feeling guilty. To be privileged, to be able to waltz in here and hope to be treated, to be able to run away from Tata Memorial, when I know lakhs of people don't have that choice. I wonder if I'm a traitor of sorts.

We walk down a bright corridor. There's a sign that says Cancer Department at the end. As we head towards it, I'm struck by a sense

of disbelief, like how can I be walking into a cancer department? It's
a fleeting thought. I am stressed because I'm wandering around in no
man's land, wondering what's going to happen next.

Well, the breast cancer department is packed. I'm in shock.
What the fuck! So many people get breast cancer?! It's like an OPD
department in a hospital. Except for one thing, there are a lot of
women with scarves around their head, or no hair, or hair that's just
growing back.

I take a deep breath.

The nurses take my details, we manage to find two chairs, and
we wait. I watch this really pretty lady with no hair walk in with her
husband. She looks healthy and happy. And not like a cancer patient.
She is smiling and talking to the nurses.

I look around, a lot of the ladies with scarves on their heads, they
seem fine. Talking to relatives, discussing things.

I guess they were on chemo. But they weren't puking or anything.
Apart from the hair loss, they seem very composed.

I didn't know what to make of it, so I just watch them.

The nurse calls our name, and we enter the doctor's chamber. The
head of the breast cancer department. Dr Mandar Nadkarni.

There's a big bear of a man sitting across the table from us, and he
looked normal. Like my age. Not an old doctor peering at me. His
desk and all the shelves behind him are filled with Ganpatis. Of every
size and kind. Playing cricket, musical instruments, lying on one side,
sitting, standing. You name it, and there's a Ganpati for it.

Anirban is talking to him about how we had gone to Tata
Memorial, and how the doctor there had recommended we see him.
He is nodding, looking at my file. Everything he does is fast. Not in a
hurried way, but in a way that felt like he was going to get this done.

The Ganpatis were obviously from patients. I'm guessing one
patient gave him a Ganpati, and then another patient saw that and
brought another one, and then it just snowballed with every patient

adding to the collection. There is also a picture of him with his wife and kids. Which is nice.

'Shormistha, we'll need to examine you.' And he yells for the nurse.

I go to the narrow examination bed, take off my T-shirt and bra, and the nurse covers me with a sheet. The curtain is pulled, and I wait for the doctor.

Where should I keep my bra?

That's what I'm worrying about. See, I always fold my T-shirt and keep the bra on top of it. Because the problem with underwire bras is they don't get all small and folded up. They pop up like brazen mammas causing a bulge under your folded T-shirt. So, I'm lying there on the narrow examination table, and my bra and T-shirt are near my knees and I'm wondering if it's weird that my hot pink bra is lying on top of my T-shirt. Should I have hidden it out of sight? Will the doctor judge me? But he heads the breast cancer department, for god's sake, what's a bra to him? It's like a spanner to a garage mechanic, or a plunger to a plumber.

My brain is going crazy. While lying there, I'm trying to manoeuvre the bra under the T-shirt, or my back, when the curtain flies open and the doctor comes in.

'Okay Shormistha, tell me what made you go see a gyneac?'

I start again with the 'I had a lump' story. He's examining me, listening. His face doesn't give anything away.

In two minutes he says, 'Okay, done. Nurse, help her change.'

And he goes back to his desk. I wear the blasted bra and the T-shirt, barely slip my feet into my laced sneakers, and all but run out. I want to know what he has to say.

'So, it is cancer. But we need to do a biopsy.'

We sit there listening to him. He's matter of fact, easy-going, quickly tells me that I have nothing to stress about. We don't even know the extent of it, so let's first find that out.

We tell him that in Tata Memorial, the biopsy will take a week at least. He's probably used to people coming for a second opinion. So, he's not rushing us, waiting for us to make up our minds.

As he talks, he writes on a prescription pad. My name, age. He pauses when I tell him forty-four.

'1973?'

I nod.

'Same year as me.'

I grin. I like him.

He keeps writing, then he makes a drawing of boobs to mark out the lump.

And dude, that drawing is perfect. I love the boobs he's drawn, they look so good. Like round jalebis that don't need a padded bra.

That clinches the deal, I love that he's given me such beautiful boobies. I make up my mind right then, and I nod at Anirban.

Anirban says, 'Can we move our treatment to you?'

And he says, 'Sure.'

That's it. I've found my doctor. I just know that Mandy (yep, in my head he's already Mandy) is the guy for me.

Mandy moves fast. He's written everything down while talking to me. I'm not crying, there's no time to cry. He's like a gust of good wind, and he's quickly outlining stuff.

Apart from the breast, there also seems to be a lymph node, in my armpit, that could be affected.

We look blank.

He explains that lymph nodes are like gatekeepers. And if one or more of them get affected, then there could be a possibility that the cancer cells have spread beyond the breast.

I take a deep breath.

He says, 'First, we'll do the biopsy and we'll know the full extent. We'll have to do a mastectomy depending on how many lumps the biopsy confirms as malignant.'

My mind starts talking to me, again.

That's your breast. They will have to remove your breast.

I know what a mastectomy is.

And what do you feel about it?

Nothing. What has to be done, has to be done. If the breast has to go, it'll go. I'm way more than one breast.

The doctor looks at me, and tells me I should consider reconstruction of the breast. It'll be done during the same surgery, right after the mastectomy.

I'm a bit numb, plus a bit full of bravado. I say no. I'll be okay without the breast. I'm a fairly confident person, I should be okay.

But this conversation isn't over.

He quickly outlines what it'll be like. There'll be no breast. Only a jagged line stitched up across the chest. A reminder, every time I look into the mirror, that I have breast cancer. And when I am better, that reminder will stay.

'Every single time you have a bath or change, you will see it.'

I ask him what do most women do.

He deftly answers that by saying, 'I ask most of them to do a reconstruction.'

He outlines the procedure. During the surgery, they scoop out all tissue etc., from inside the affected breast. Think of it like making stuffed baingan. They leave the flap or skin of the breast intact. Then they'll take tissue from my abdomen or back, and fill the breast with that tissue and stitch the flap back up. And voila, the breast is back. With my own tissue.

I ask him, 'What are the negatives?'

Surgery will take longer, and recovering from the surgery will also take longer.

'You'll keep me in hospital longer?'

'Yes.'

Then I don't want it. I don't want to be in the hospital for a day more than I need to.

I tell the doctor that I don't think I'll opt for reconstruction. I'm okay the way I am.

He tells me to think about it, and that he absolutely recommends it. He looks at Anirban, who nods as well.

That's it. Just another easy-peasy day, where you are asked if you want your breast reconstructed or not.

I mean, how has my life changed so fast? How am I going to be sure that I make the right decision?

Ughhh. Till a couple of days back, at this time, I'd be in the office, debating over what to order for lunch. Rolls or fish thali? Khichdi or bhurji? And now it's suddenly reached, breast or no breast. I feel a pang of envy. Why am I here, when everyone else is going about their usual routine?

Mandy hands us the prescription, with the beautiful boobies drawn on it, and tells us to go to the biopsy floor. He adds, 'If they say they can't do it today, tell them I asked for it today itself.'

Just that one sentence, and I feel better again. Mentally stronger and sorted. How do I explain this? It's such a small thing, but that moment when you're lost and don't know where to go, and who to turn to, to find a doctor who just takes over is incredible. Who doesn't just make you feel you are a patient, but a person. Who's like a cyclone that just sweeps in and gets everything done. Who isn't one for wasting any time at all. His tone is casual when he says tell them I asked for it today. But I can tell he means business, and he's going to speed this up. I realize I could not have found anyone better.

He also says that I need to have a PET scan the next day.

PET scan? Both Anirban and I stare at him blankly.

I don't know if he's relieved or surprised to have patients who don't have a degree in oncology, but he calmly explains that a PET scan is to check if the cancer has spread anywhere in your body. If some stray cells have managed to escape the lymph node gatekeepers, and attach themselves to another organ.

Just writing this gives me the shivers. Hearing him say that was like someone threw ice-cold water on all my positivity.

It's like I was on a see-saw, up and down in seconds.

Mandy is super matter of fact. And empathetic at the same time. And I think that helps. He's already telling me that lots of women get breast cancer. And more importantly, lots of women beat it. The only issue will be that my life will be on pause. I'm young, healthy, and there's no point worrying about what I don't know.

Something about his manner which has no fake sympathy, but states only the facts, helps me.

I'll do what he tells me to do.

We thank him. And we walk out.

In the corridor we turn to each other. We both liked him. And most importantly, he's got this show on the road.

Ziba: All okay?

Me: Yes. Btw this doctor said if last year, the gyneac had made me do a sonomammography instead of just a sonography, they might have caught it in a pre-cancer stage. Damn.

Doctor seems nice. I liked him.

Results will come by quickly.

Lots of ladies here with no hair. But they all look sweet 😊 I will look stupid 🙁

The biopsy appointment. As predicted, they say all appointments for the day are full, and we'll have to come back tomorrow. We whip out the prescription, and tell them that Dr Mandar has said it must be done today. Ha! The change in expression. Obviously Mandy is a dude here, and no one says no to him.

We hang around a bit, and then they tell us they'll squeeze me in.

I'm not scared of injections, so I'm not fretting. I vaguely remember my biopsy as a teenager. They inserted a thin needle into the lump. Or that's what I remember of it.

They call my name. I fill in various forms. And then I'm taken to a makeshift back room. The front part is a general storage area kind of place. And then behind the curtain-partition is a narrow bed with some machines around it. I take off my bra and T-shirt. This time I stuff the bra under the T-shirt. They put a sheet on me and then I wait.

A lady arrives. She tells me she'll give me mild local anaesthesia. I am relieved.

She comes back in two minutes, all set. Arranges her tools and takes out a thin needle.

I'm cool.

Then she takes out the biopsy needle. A fat bugger with what looks like a crochet needle attached to it. I am horrified. Not enough to leap out and run, but yes, I close my eyes.

Okay, before I go further, here's the thing. I like blood and gore. It doesn't freak me out. I'm just curious. And I've always wanted to attend a surgery, and touch a heart or a liver or a brain. No, not lungs and kidneys for some reason. I don't find them that appealing on the organ-touching scale.

But yes, a heart and brain would be gooey to touch and sort of pulpy. Like slime or Play-Doh.

Remember the time my dog bit my nose? I had a tear, which a plastic surgeon had to stitch up. Now, the fun part of a surgery where you don't need to go under general anaesthesia, and where they only have to put five tiny stitches on you, is they let you walk to the OT complex. Which in this case was a whole floor. As I was walking to my OT, I saw an operation happening in one of the rooms I was passing. Before anyone could say, 'Pass me the forceps', or whatever it is they shout, I had opened the door, and was walking in. They had a TV screen kind of thing, where the surgery was being broadcast, and before I could stand there transfixed, the ward boys and nurses hauled me out.

I like all this stuff.

I just wasn't sure if I like it on me.

And when I saw that biopsy needle, I was like, 'Okay then, classify this under non-enjoyable activities.'

She gives me the local anaesthesia with that thin needle. It doesn't hurt at all. Then she waits, and before you know it, I see her pick up her biopsy gun. I turn my face, grit my teeth, and tell myself there's going to be a lot of needles coming up in the next few months, so I better get my shit together.

And then, boom, I feel like someone just stapled my boob. It hurts. And it had to be done thrice.

I'm now in a tearing hurry to get out of the hospital. The doctor gives me a mild pain medication, and tells me to sleep it off.

I head home. I'm tired, I reek of the hospital, and I keep thinking what if they had caught this the year before. The oncologist's words keep going around in my head. Maybe if they had done a sono-mammography a year back, they might have caught it at the pre-cancer stage.

I shake myself. There's no point in thinking about what could have been. I just have to focus on what's coming now.

The phone pings. It's Dr Rohatgi, the doctor Tarini spoke about. He's free to talk just now.

I call him, give him a quick outline of my case. He listens patiently. And tells me, you need to go where you feel good. This is not a time to feel guilty. Tata Memorial is a great hospital, but if it's taking time, and you like Kokilaben and your doctor, then go for it.

That's all I need to hear. So Kokilaben it will be, to see me through to the other side.

14

ω

I'm up bright and early. It's the day of the PET scan. My chief cheerleader, Oinx, is coming with Anirban and me. I try to tell her that she doesn't have to come, but there's no shaking her off as usual. And I'm glad for that.

The evening before, we made an appointment for the PET scan. And that's when we discovered it comes under the Department of Nuclear Medicine. More than being scared, my mind boggles with what that could mean. There are 'radioactive area' stickers plastered all over. It's late evening, so the place is pretty empty. And we beg, and we use Dr Mandar's name liberally, and land a 10 a.m. appointment.

So, here's the thing with hospitals and appointments. Always take the first one if you can. Because it's pretty much a domino effect. And it has nothing in common with the pizza chain except that Indian Standard Time is as stretchable as the bloody cheese on a thin crust.

One person turns up late, and it just cascades from there. Your 4 p.m. appointment will never happen before 6 p.m., at the earliest.

Also, people, once they walk into the doctor's chamber, never want to come out. I mean, how can you have so many questions? Is the entire family giving the MBBS exam?

97

I realize that I have a condition called 'Brain Freeze and Overcompensation'. Which means all I can do is nod vigorously and smile like I'm meeting Shah Rukh Khan and not the doctor, and that's not the ideal way to know more about your condition. But there's also a limit to how you can get an encyclopaedia worth of information in every meeting.

I've seen patients ask the doctor just about everything, except their credit card CVV number. Have they not heard of Google? Or is it just overenthusiastic class participation?

My theory is when you pay, you want to juice everything, and in this case the doctor must give you the entire PhD on the illness. And then of course you'll refute it with what your neighbour or uncle or second cousin has told you. It's a wonder doctors don't just inject families with a drug that stops them from speaking.

Anyway, we didn't get the first appointment, but 10 a.m. is still relatively early. The person at the counter tells me it'll take under two hours. I'm thinking we should be done by noon latest.

The reason I'm calculating all this is because I can't eat anything before the PET scan. And I'm the kind who can't live without food. As soon as I wake up, I want to eat. It's an old habit, which started because of, take one guess … yes, my old friend, stress.

When I first started working, I was living in a PG in Calcutta. My PG package included rent for a bed in a double-sharing room, and three meals. One of which would be packed for office lunch. Except it didn't really qualify as lunch. On most days it was watery aloo ki sabzi and two slices of bread with margarine and salt and pepper on them. Slight Oliver Twist scenes here in our charming little boarding house.

What that meant was I hardly ate. Especially since breakfast was usually the same thing, but minus the aloo ki sabzi. And dinner was nice, but served from 8 to 8.30 p.m., and I rarely made it back from work by then.

As a result, I fell very sick, and a kindly doctor described it as the start of ulcers. He also, in great detail, described an endoscopy where they put a camera down your throat to check out your insides. And I think he did such a good job that I became a convert. I made sure my stomach was never empty. I got up in the morning and ate; in fact, I furiously ate and nibbled almost all the time.

That's why this not eating was stressing me. Anyway, the three of us were in the hospital bright and early. I am excited because I get to meet a colleague and friend at the hospital who has some blood tests to run. Shaoli is my most kick-ass friend, who has had thalassemia since she was a kid. Which means she needs to go for transfusions every fifteen days. But the thing is, Shaoli is also an energizer bunny. She will never let thalassemia or hospitals or transfusions get in her way. She does all her hospital visits on her own, with her trusty Kindle, and scares the hell out of the nurses and attendants with her efficiency. When I got diagnosed, her name was the first one that popped in my head with the hashtag #BeLikeShaoli. I was going to take inspiration from her, and treat this as a minor irritant and nothing more.

The best part was all her hospital stuff happened at Kokilaben. This meant I had insider tips, like 'Make sure your Kindle is always charged', 'Grab a coffee at the Starbucks before everything starts', 'If you make friends with the bedding guy, he'll give you an extra pillow, and the blood test people are fantastic.'

Which was awesome. Because before my PET scan, I have to do a whole bunch of blood tests. I meet Shaoli at the hospital, and it feels like a little party at the Blood Collection department. The blood people stare at my arm in horror. The hospital near my home had botched it up and I had black bruises all over my arm. Shaoli, of course, with the authority of someone who's been doing this for years, informs me that they are called track marks.

The blood people … hold on a second … what do you call people who collect blood? Blood collectors? Blood service providers? Blood experts? Vampires? Anyway, these guys are super-efficient, the blood tests happened smoothly and then it is time to go to the basement and the Department of Nuclear Medicine.

The place is nothing like it had been the evening before. It is packed. Patients and their caregivers are spilling out of every chair possible. My heart sinks. This is going to be a long wait.

We manage to find two chairs, and Anirban and Oinx keep playing musical chairs while I settle into one. I open my Kindle, but I read nothing. Instead, I watch the patients and their families. There is a young girl with long hair, who is also going to take the test. If you look at her, you'd never imagine something is wrong. Heck, if you look at me, you'd never imagine there is cancer inside me.

Finally, at 12 noon, Anirban goes to the counter. Turns out there is something wrong with the machine, and today is exceptionally chaotic. There is nothing to be done.

See that's why hospitals charge you a bomb. Because they are like Deepak Chopra, teaching you valuable life lessons. Like acceptance and resignation. There's no point fretting because it'll only happen when it's meant to happen.

But lucky for me he comes back with forms. Where I have to declare that if I die during the procedure, the hospital will not be responsible.

Whatever!

After another forty-five minutes of waiting and wondering when I'd start feeling hungry, they call my name. I am ushered into a room, where I meet a doctor seated behind a large table. He asks me questions, checks if I am liable to cop it on the table, and then explains how radioactive it is.

Duh! Saw the big hazard sign all over and made the connection, doctor.

And then, with a final flourish he tells me that there could be side effects. Like loose motions, irritation, skin rashes, etc. Just the usual kind of pleasantries one exchanges before a scan.

Finally, I am called in. The first thing they do is attach a big multipronged plug-like thing that's connected to a needle that goes straight into my vein. Then I am packed off to a closet-like room, to change.

I slip into the cream kurta pyjama set, with tiny yellow flowers on it. Not my style, but what the hell, in life you have to be open to other sartorial influences. And this one is part of a collection that I label in my head as the Spring Summer Hospital Runway.

I wait some more, glad to have my Kindle for company.

And then I am called in one final time. The attendant tells me to leave my backpack with my caregivers, and I protest hugely. The backpack is my security blanket. I need something old, something that is mine that I can hold on to.

He patiently explains to me, 'Apke brain ko total rest mangta hai.' Which means for the next hour and a half, no phone, no specs, no Kindle, and no books. Damn, what on earth am I going to do?

I promise him I will not use my phone or read, but I'd like to keep my backpack with me. He relents and ushers me into a room. It is dark, and there are three huge La-Z-Boy recliners, and a fluffy blanket in each. I kid you not, some popcorn and I would have thought I'm at a personal movie screening where they take blood instead of tickets.

I settle down. Put the blanket on my legs. A lady comes in and injects two big syringes of liquids into me. I'm guessing this is the radioactive stuff they put in your body. Because I have done some last-minute googling!

The PET scan is basically when they inject some radioactive material into your body. It accumulates near the organs and gives off gamma rays. Special cameras then pick this up, and perform imaging.

Okay, it's more complex, but this is the nuclear medicine for dummies version.

They also give you a big bottle of clear liquid to drink. It is labelled Oral Contra, which I am guessing is the dye. And now you sit back on the La-Z-Boy, under your fluffy blanket, and sip this bottle empty in the next sixty minutes. So chill, so fancy!

Except every ten minutes I have to pee. And I keep wondering if I put off the lights in the loo, will my radioactive pee glow in the dark? But because I don't really care for public bathrooms, I don't carry out this scientific research.

Through all this, the room is silent, and in between the door opens twice, and two shadowy figures enter. One of them settles beside me. I peer at them, the one away from me is the young girl I had seen at the reception. The lady next to me is middle aged, or at least that's what I can tell in the dark. It is odd, to be bound together in that tiny, dark room, by something that we have no control over, that could change our lives, for a while or forever.

The lady next to me breaks the silence by asking why I am here. I tell her, and then make the mistake of asking why she is here. The reason I say I made a mistake, because in a cancer ward, you quickly realize that you shouldn't ask what you can't handle. She's had throat cancer, and she is wearing a wig. My heart sinks. She is sweet, and speaks to me in a whisper, telling me about how difficult it has been for her for a year to eat solid food. She talks about her surgeries, the pipe in her throat, chemotherapy. And I wonder if I have understood the magnitude of what is happening to me. I tuck the thought aside, and cling on to what the oncologist had told me the day before. That breast cancer is the most curable form of cancer. That it would inconvenience me, and put my life on hold, but a large number of women, and men, recover from it, and lead great lives post their treatment.

I swear that I will not ask anyone why they are here, or what's wrong with them. I didn't have the mental strength to deal with it.

Finally, after sixty minutes, someone comes to call me. I pick up my bag and walk into a huge room, with another glass room next to it. Like a sound studio. In the big room is a machine, which looks like a slightly less claustrophobic version of the MRI machine. In the other room are the technicians.

I put my backpack on the solitary chair in the room, remove my sneakers, and clamber on. They strap me in, instruct me to stay still. And before I can freak out, I am in that round hole.

I slide in, this time on my back. I remember a trick I had read about years back when I had anxiety attacks. The trick is to basically picture a happy place in your head and retreat there. In my head it's always been a green clearing in a forest. When I was a teenager, my father was posted to Shillong. And we lived right next to a forest. I'd often walk here, smelling the pine trees, picking up pine cones, breathing the sharp, clean air. My happy place in my head looked a lot like that. Except, it had sunlight and even a stream gurgling somewhere.

I am okay. My head is in the happy place, I am calm, and actually this doughnut-shaped machine is not that bad. It's more compact, so when they slide you in, your head pops out from the other side. They take me back and forth a couple of times, and then it is showtime.

They had warned me when the medicine activated I would feel warm. Well, I am in the centre of the machine, there is pin-drop silence. And suddenly I think I have peed in my pyjamas. My mind mildly panics as I experience a warm feeling creeping down my legs. My first thought is '*Halleluiah, I got the loosies on the PET scan machine. Yikes. Who is going to clean it, and how will I get off? And then ... wait a second, I think I peed, it's so warm ...*'

While my brain is reeling, the warmth is quickly spreading to my hands and feet.

Okay, it's not pee. It's the radioactive shit.

The attendant comes in and says, 'ho gaya'. And that was it. I am unstrapped and out of there like a shot. They keep me in a waiting area for thirty minutes to check for side effects.

Luckily, apart from feeling like my mouth is metallic, I am fine. Also, I had read somewhere that there have been instances of people setting off alarms at airport scanners after a PET scan. Would be a cool party trick, if it weren't the scariest thing ever.

To know that you've been diagnosed with breast cancer is one thing. To do a test that'll tell you if the cancer cells have leaked into other parts of your body is something else. You wonder how much strength you have.

I go for a late lunch at 3.30 p.m. with Oinx. Anirban has to leave for office. Over lunch, Oinx tells me Ziba and she have started a WhatsApp group, and some of my other friends have also joined, so they can all know what's happening with me. Without having to disturb Anirban.

It feels strange. A WhatsApp group about me, without me!

I beg and plead with her to give me the link and let me join. When she refuses to relent, with a side helping of pasta, I dish out my Brahmastra: 'I have cancer, and all I want to do is join one group, and you are going to say no to that?'

And just like that, I'm in!

15

ᘛᘚ

22 March

4.56 p.m.

Oinx added Shormistha

Ziba: Thanks Oinx.

Oinx: That idiot Shorms is also now a part of the group.

Ziba: Shormeeeee … wanting to know everything …

Oinx: Please vote if you want her chucked out.

Ziba: Who allowed u in 😄

Oinx: She bullied me to let her in 🙆

Gauri: Haha. Of course she did. She'll want to be on top of things 😎

Oinx: Yeah what a control freak man!!!

Ziba: 😃 😃

Oinx: Now we can't bitch about her 🤗

Gauri: Hehe

Ziba: So there is Gauri, Oinx, Vidhya, Ziba, Roohi, and now the bully herself.

Oinx: You can vote to have her chucked out.

Ziba: Did she herself suggest that too?? 😆😆

Gauri: Kiski majaal.

Ziba: Correct …

Oinx: You think she wants to get chucked out of any place ever?! 😎

Shormistha: Helloo. How can you keep me out? I would have cried all night.

Ziba: Hellllo darling.

Shormistha: 😚

Shormistha: Yay! I am part of the group now.

Oindrilla: Ziba we will start a separate group without her 😂😂😂

Gauri: Nobody would dare 😄

Ziba: For today … the secret vote is happening on another group.

Shormistha: Coff coff

Ziba: So today you were the PET star? Back home? Take rest now. Get off the phone.

Shormistha: We are outside. Just finished eating. Anirban had to go, Oinx is with me. Have to give blood again. Then done for the day and the weekend! 💃💃💃💃 You guys better treat me like a normal person okay. I want movies, cycling, and everything else.

16

ω

And that's what I did. Tried very hard to lead a normal life for the next few days. As things started moving at breakneck speed, I tried to cling on to regular stuff even tighter. In my head I started referring to my life as BC, or Before Cancer. And AD, After Diagnoses.

Shiny, my awesome friend and colleague, who was always calm and effortlessly easy to be around, cycled with me every day. She listened to stories of my doctor visits, without exclaiming or behaving like I was going to either pop it or break down. It was a relief to be able to tell someone about my rather strange days, and discuss it so normally, over cutting chai breaks while cycling.

Actually, all my friends behaved normal around me. Plus, I had decided to put the news out on social media. Yep, control freak. Let me put it out before others start talking about it. I did think a lot about the hashtag I was going to use.

Now, it might sound weird that I've been diagnosed with cancer and am doing a PET scan, and I'm thinking about a hashtag! But that's how I am. Writing is therapy for me, and in this case, I was determined I'm going to be honest and tell it like it is. This was my journey. And however ugly it got, I would observe it, and then examine it by writing about it.

And the more I examined it in those couple of blurry, hectic days, the more convinced I was, that I am not here to beat the shit out of cancer or to tell it to fuck off. I was here to listen to it, to learn from it, and once I understand the things it wants to tell me, it will leave. Yes, I was fighting, but I was fighting the good fight. And I would win, if I treated it with respect.

#DealsWithCancer. I settled on that. It didn't say anything violent. It just said that I would work my way through this thing.

Of course, the flip side to putting your life up for public consumption was that some friends would call me, super agitated, and ask why they had to see the news on social media. And why they didn't hear it from me.

Dude, it's not like it's my daughter's wedding. And I have been calling everyone, and missed inviting you. No. It's because I have cancer, and maybe I was thinking about myself. For a change!

And the second thing that happens is everyone wants to know who my oncologist is. And everyone knows someone who'll know him, and can tell us if he's good or not.

I am going blue in the face saying I like him. But apparently that's not good enough. So, I start throwing his resume at them. He was with Tata Memorial for ten years, he's a professor of surgical oncology, every website says he's the best for breast cancer.

But no, everyone has to do a reference check on him. And then call me back and say they are happy to hear he's good. But that's what I was telling you the first time around!

And of course, everyone had some friend/relative/chacha/bhateeja who knows him, and promised they'll put in a word for me.

It was super embarrassing because the next time I met Mandy, he said, 'I've got at least four calls, telling me about you.' Ugh.

While I'm dealing with this, I'm also dealing with something that's tearing me up. My parents. Dad can hardly come to the phone, he starts crying as soon as he hears my voice. Mom is the brave one, but I can tell they are going through hell. By now they are flooded with advice. Which doesn't always make it easy, especially when you are in a different city.

I'm feeling terrible for them, but I'm trying to keep my mind on the practical stuff, and not get washed away by the emotional tsunami.

In fact, the first oncologist tells me something that I latch on to. She tells me, 'You just have to focus on yourself. The next couple of months of your life, you have to be the most important person in your life.'

I'm not that kind of person, but something in what she says stays with me. That night after the PET test, I'm tired, exhausted, but I sit down and I think.

All my life I have trusted the voice in my head. Every time I've gone against my instinct, things have gone wrong. Now more than ever, I have to trust that voice. I have to listen to myself. I have to find what's correct for me.

And I have to put myself first. My getting better is the only thing I should focus on, everything else will be secondary.

I also, in Amitabh Bachchan's words, use a lifeline. I call Himanshu, my one and only friend who has had cancer, and beaten it.

Actually, from that point onwards I started realizing that there are signs. Like the universe had been scattering them all over for a year or two, and now they were coming together, and all I had to do was look for them, and follow them.

Only three months back, I had gone to Goa, and spent two weeks chilling with my folks. Maybe we were meant to have that time together, before this hit us. Similarly, my friendship with Himanshu happened out of the blue. I attended a heritage walk, and out of the fourteen people on the walk together, for some reason we got talking. And that's it. With time, we became friends. He was much younger than me and he had just recovered from cancer. In fact, that was his first outing after his treatment. I found him very wise for his age, and was fascinated with how he had dealt with something so big.

And guess what, the universe planted him in my path. I call him, bring him up to date on my meeting with Mandy, and then tell him to give me advice.

He tells me three very important things. Do what you think is best for you, there'll be lots of advice, you listen to your body. Eat everything you can before chemo, stuff your face with your favourite food. And finally, follow only your doctor's advice.

This is all practical stuff, and I am feeling like I'll be able to handle it.

What I don't know is that I'm still in denial. I'm thinking this will not be that bad. The doctor sounded very calm. Chances are they'll manage to get out the lump, and I'll just have to go through some radiation to doubly make sure all the cancer cells have been eradicated. I feel good, I look good, I don't think it can be that bad.

I don't say it.

But at the back of my mind, I am terrified of chemotherapy.

Not of the cancer, not of the mastectomy, but of this.

And of course, everyone's first question to me is, 'Will you have to go through chemotherapy?' And the tone they use is, 'Will you be bungee jumping without a cord?' When I tell them that I'm not sure, they get saucer-eyed.

I can see gloom and doom imprinted in their voice.

I am scared.

My parents are telling me about a friend whose daughter went through a hellish experience. Himanshu tells me he didn't want to eat anything, and he was tired all the time.

Chemotherapy.

My hair will fall off. I'll be nauseous at the sight of food. I'll feel sick all the time.

I start remembering all the books and movies I've watched. One minute! I can't remember a single book or movie where the person who has cancer doesn't die! Shit. From *Love Story* to *The Fault in Our Stars*.

And every single Hindi movie.

First, they get diagnosed with cancer, then they start wearing kurta pyjamas if they are men, and white clothes if they are women. Next, their friends and relatives don't tell them they are going to die, but they stand exactly one foot away from them and cry and sing sad songs. So, I'm not sure how the patient doesn't guess it's bad, and realize that they are probably going to die.

Also, if the doctor tells the patient that they are going to die, then the patient doesn't tell his family. And insists on being extra cheerful, while singing sad songs. And the patient is so extra that I don't know how the family doesn't understand something is totally wrong with the person.

Either way, it always seems like someone is going to die.

I start thinking that the world is divided into two kinds of people. Those who would want to know they are dying, and those who would not. Which one am I?

Since the doctor didn't say anything to me, that night, before I sleep, I turn to Anirban and seriously ask him, 'If the doctor has told you I am dying, please tell me.' He looks at me like I have lost it. And thankfully doesn't break into a sad song.

So, I presume, that it's going to be okay.

In fact, I presume, it's going to be one lump, and they'll get it out. I'm sipping a cocktail called Hoping Like Hell, and the ingredients are some parts optimism, some parts denial.

I also take the time to think about whether I want reconstruction or not. When I say take my time, that's probably an exaggeration, because I only have less than forty-eight hours to decide. I never question the fact that I will have to lose my breast. In fact, I am so eager to get the cancer out, that I totally take it in my stride. No second thoughts at all. But this, I'm wondering what to do.

I worry about how my T-shirts and tops will look. One breast there, and one not there. I search online. There are mastectomy bras and swimming costumes. There are even silicon breasts that you can put in your bra, and it looks exactly like your real breast.

Also, I don't want to undergo any more surgery than I have to. The oncologist has indicated that it will be a long surgery if I opt for the reconstruction.

Anirban, Oinx and Ziba think I should do it. It'll help me mentally. I discuss it with my parents. Dad is too distraught to give good advice. Mom is beside herself with worry, and doesn't want me to even go through one extra procedure or surgery. She's clear that it's a no.

I just can't decide what to do. Wait a minute, what happens to my beautiful La Senza bras? The ones I spent a fortune on? Damn.

I have another worry. And that is my pets, Milo and Tuggu. Himanshu had told me that just as his cancer treatment started to get over, his dog fell sick and died. He felt like his dog took the illness off him.

Guess what? I googled, and found there were many people who echoed the same thing.

I decided the best thing to do was to talk to the dog and the cat, separately. Tell them what was wrong with me, and then also tell them that I would deal with this, and come through.

It was a successful heart-to-heart. Because Milo, my dog, yawned in my face. And Tuggu, my cat, fell asleep while I was talking to him.

I took that to be a good sign. If the animals were chill, then there was nothing to worry about.

A day later, I walk into the house with an envelope. It has the PET scan result. My heart is not just in my mouth, it's everywhere, in my shaking hands, head, shivering knees. What if I never open it? What if I throw it away and run?

Anirban patiently waits for me to open it. I sit on the floor, slowly take out the report from the envelope, my eyes scan everything quickly. I don't care a shit about what's written there, I just want to see what's at the end.

The cancer is limited to the breast. The lymph nodes have done their job.

I start crying while holding Anirban. I have never been happier.

It's strange how your life and the circumstances change. Ten days back I was crying because I got diagnosed with breast cancer.

And tonight, I'm drinking wine and crying and celebrating because I only have breast cancer.

17
ω

The next day is hospital day again.

I'm already thinking I've made more visits to the hospital in the last few days than I have in my life.

In fact, my biggest dread is hospitals. I just want to flee when I see them. And a big part of that is the white tube lights that are mandatory in almost every hospital.

That white light is soul sucking. It reminds me of all sorts of things. Not having done homework, and more importantly, remembering on a Sunday night that it needs to be submitted the next day.

Sitting in my hostel room, as evening turns to dusk, and realizing that I don't fit in, that I picked the wrong subject to study.

Taking a bus from office, in a city that I've just moved to, and not recognizing a single street or face.

Turning a white tube light on is like flooding your brain with depressing memories.

I have this habit of walking around neighbourhoods, and staring at people's houses. #StalkerAlert. The windows where you see yellow lights, I imagine a cosy lamp, books, people talking and laughing, chai and samosas.

The windows where I see white lights, I imagine a cot, with a man in a vest and white pyjamas that are no longer white. And his wife is in the kitchen, and clothes and wet towels are strewn all over, and the TV is on, with a rather vile news channel blaring away.

Such is my hatred for tube lights.

Though truth be told Kokilaben Hospital doesn't seem that bad. Our appointment is in the evening, and today, Ziba is coming along with Anirban and me.

She has quickly wrapped a film project in Bengaluru and come back to Mumbai this morning. All the while she's been pinging me, saying she hates the fact that she's not in town. And the first thing she's doing is coming to the hospital with me.

I'm glad to have her company. Ziba is my most sorted friend. The best practical advice, amazing organizational skills, and also being Parsi, she has the funniest stories ever. If you're sick, you want her on your team. And the icing on this Parsi cake was that Ziba knew people who had breast cancer, and who recovered and were leading great lives. So, she came into the scene, knowing that we could do this.

After much hugging and greeting and gawking at the wonders of Kokilaben, we step into the cancer department. To meet the boss, my oncologist. Today is when I'll know what's going to happen next.

But before that I'm meeting an oncologist with an exotic name. Tarini's family doctor, who told me to stop feeling guilty about being privileged and to focus on getting treated fast, said he knows her, and that I should meet her with my case papers.

We troop upstairs to the cancer department, and after the mandatory waiting, and coffee, and staring at all the ladies without hair and wondering if that will be my fate, we get called into her room.

She's beautiful. We hand her my file, and I'm fascinated as I stare at her. She's well-dressed, has immaculately done nails, and looks my age or younger.

I tell her Dr Rohatgi has asked us to get in touch with her. She asks if my operation is done. I say no. She looks puzzled, but opens the file.

I think she was wondering why we were here. Because we were looking at her, as if she's going to give us the answer to life's biggest mysteries.

She asks if I've met Dr Mandar Nadkarni with this report. I say no. She explains that he's the head of the breast cancer department and a surgical oncologist. Which means he's going to operate on me, and also decide my protocol.

Protocol?

As she explains, I realize that's cancer parlance for your treatment plan.

I roll it around in my head. Such a military word. I've heard my father using the word. A prescribed way to do things. I feel strangely comforted. Like my childhood and what was happening to me right now collided, and this was a sign. A good sign.

In the course of my treatment, I realize that it's one sure-shot way to identify a family or person who has seen cancer: they know the vocabulary. They understand PET, the much-coveted NED (No Evidence of Disease), protocol, onco surgeon, etc.

Initially it fazes you, every term just reminds you how vulnerable you are.

But slowly, the terms become familiar friends. And you use them in your conversations all the time. And then, those closest to you also start to use it. And other cancer survivors or caregivers, when they talk to you, you all comfortably use the vocabulary like a secret club code that binds you. Like the P language of your childhood. Only this one is fraught with tears and worry and pain, but also joy and learning and so much loving.

So, she's not going to have anything to do with my treatment?

She shakes her head. The hierarchy of cancer doctors is dawning on me. The onco surgeons are the big daddies. The scalpel wielding bad boys, or girls are like the commander-in-chief of this battle. The medical oncos are the second-in-command. They handle the troops, which is the chemotherapy.

When the surgical onco goes in all guns blazing, and takes the enemy by surprise, the medical oncos come in and unleash the foot soldiers, and then there's hand-to-hand combat.

They all swear allegiance to the onco surgeons.

Okay, so that's why she's wondering why we're meeting her before the onco surgeon.

Awkward much.

Ask her something, maybe about the chemo.

But I don't think I'll need chemo.

Dude, you paid one and a half thousand bucks for this appointment, ask her something, anything.

'Err … will you be my doctor if I have to get chemo?'

'Dr Mandar will decide that.'

'Okay, so what's chemo like?'

She settles back. And tells me chemotherapy is a necessary thing and there's no need to be scared of it. The only thing is to be careful. To make sure I wash everything well, to avoid crowds, to stay away from people, so I don't risk infection.

I'm grinning. This is Mumbai, how will I avoid crowds? Plus, I tell her that I'm cycling every day, weaving through crowded lanes. She looks horrified. She's very clear that sanitizing everything, masking up, not eating fruits without peeling them, and avoiding pollution are essential.

I nod my head vigorously. We say thank you and step out. Ziba pokes me in the ribs and says, 'I know you are not going to do any of that. You're going to eat rubbish and keep cycling, but you better listen.'

We now wait for Mandy. A little reverentially, now that we know he's going to head my show. I'm still hoping like hell that there's no chemotherapy. How will I ever lead the life that doctor just described? Ziba promises me a new 100-rupee note if there's no chemo.

The waiting room is buzzing, the doctor has started seeing patients. Now here's the thing. The nurses have created a super simple device to manage the crowds. There are three or four rooms blocked for him. I've seen two, and both have a profusion of Ganpatis. Now if I'm with the doctor in one room, the next patient is ushered into another room, and by the time the patients take out their files etc., the doctor walks into this room, and in the meantime another room already has other patients ushered in. So, the doctor is like this chess player who is playing against multiple people simultaneously. I think it's too cool.

Anyway, we walk into one of the rooms, put my PET scan and the biopsy report on the table. The doctor comes in like a mini cyclone. He's in his blue scrubs.

He says hello to us, is pleased that the reports have arrived quickly, and takes a look at them.

'So, the good news is that the PET scan shows it's restricted to the breast.'

Uh ho, anyone who says, 'So the good news is . . .', will always follow it up with a but or bad news.

'But the bad news is, it's gone to the lymph nodes.'

My gatekeepers!

A siren is pinging in my brain.

This isn't good. The first oncologist who saw me said if it hasn't reached the lymph nodes, we're good, we can handle this easily. But if it's gone to the lymph nodes, then it's far more serious.

Mandy is looking at me. My eyes must be one big question mark.

He lays out everything. One big lymph node lit up in the PET scan, so they can't take a chance. There might be other lymph nodes that are infected as well. Even with that one infected lymph node, they can't risk it.

They will have to do a mastectomy, and then chemotherapy and radiation.

You could have cut through the silence with a butter knife.

I can't get myself to look away from the report lying in front of me, because I'm scared I'll start crying.

I hear Anirban asking, 'She will need chemotherapy? Are you sure?'

The doctor gently explains that if this had been detected before my lymph node had been infected, then maybe, just maybe, they could have just given me radiation. But now, there was always a possibility that something could have leaked past the lymph node, and so they were not going to take any chances. They'd have to consider a protocol that can save me from things we might not have spotted or a future relapse.

(Can I just pause to tell you how hard it is to even write the word relapse? Even writing it here, just putting it down in words, makes me want to abandon everything I'm doing, and curl up like a ball and howl my head off.)

I still can't believe this is happening. It's no longer a simple procedure, this is a shit storm. I've never faced something like this in my life. I am not prepared for this, I want to yell. Instead, I just sit there, with a half-smile on my face.

The doctor gently and slowly goes on. The lump in my breast is very close to the nipple, so they will have to sacrifice the nipple.

There, another word.

Why did he use the word 'sacrifice'?

Because you'll have to give up your breast, if you want to get okay.

I'm okay with that. I think so. I just want this damn cancer out of me.

But the nipple?

The doctor is talking to me, I try and still my mind and listen to him.

He's explaining that if it was just one malignant lump, they might have gone towards breast conservation, and opted for a lumpectomy or partial removal of the breast. But in my case, the biopsy shows one confirmed lump, one suspicious one, and some calcification. So, they'll want to take the whole breast out to minimize risk.

It's the best thing to do. And I should opt for reconstruction.

My eyes widen.

He looks at me and says, 'I hope you're going to do the reconstruction?'

Till the minute he asked me that question, even I didn't know what I wanted. Yet, I hear myself say yes.

He looks very pleased.

The tissue will most probably come from below my shoulder blade. And when they retain the flap or the outer skin of my breast, they'll take out the nipple. They'll graft some skin from the same tissue area, and stitch it over where the nipple used to be.

Ohkay.

'But if you take tissue from my shoulder blade, is there anything I will not be able to do?'

'Climb trees.'

That's decided then. I'm forsaking my career as a toddy tapper, and going ahead and getting the reconstruction done. I grin.

The doctor is so pleased at my decision, he tells us the breast will look absolutely natural, no one will be able to tell. And he takes out his phone and starts showing us headless pictures of women's torsos and their boobs, asking us to guess which one is reconstructed.

We're taken aback for a moment, and then enthusiastically take part in the guessing game.

It was fun. A bit like a hospital version of Bangkok.

He then tells me to go downstairs and get an appointment with Dr Quazi, who is the plastic surgeon. He adds that I should ask the plastic surgeon to call him once he sees me, because then he'll plan my surgery.

We collect my file and go out. I look at Ziba. I'm not getting that new 100-rupee note.

My eyes fill up with tears. Ziba and Anirban hug me. I can tell they are as affected as me, but are doing their best to cheer me up.

18
ω

*I*knew that now we're staring down a strange tunnel. And you would now have to go through a really hard time.

I know you were still hoping for it to be a lighter version.

But I had a feeling since the first time we met the oncologist at Tata Memorial that it wouldn't be that. I was just preparing for the worst. While you were trying to keep your sanity intact, by hoping for the less painful way.

I would feel terrible. Seeing that you were still hopeful.

—Anirban

19

ᗯ

9.30 p.m.

Ziba: Friends of Shorms, status is this ... I was with her at docs visit last evening. She has DCIS grade 3 ... which means the cancer is non-invasive (v good news) but within non-invasive grade 3 is the highest grade. There was also a lymph node that lit up.

Gauri: But totally removable, right?

Ziba: Yes removable, but doc wants to be careful and go all out. Surgery, chemo and radiation. She took the chemo news a little badly ... she wasn't expecting to have to do chemo ... but knowing Shorms, she will bounce back.

20

(⌣)

The next few days were manic.

Not just because before I knew it I would be wheeled into surgery, but because I had so many things to deal with. Mentally and just in terms of my life.

I realized that my life would change completely over the next few months. Much as I was declaring I'd still go to the office during my chemo, and I'd still cycle, I knew that just meeting doctors and getting tests done was exhausting. Surgery and chemo would be climbing Mount Everest-level tiring.

That evening, when my oncologist served me the entire cancer buffet as part of my treatment plan, that was probably the hardest night for me. Like I said earlier, through all the tests and diagnoses and doctor visits, I was sleeping like a baby. It's like my body already knew that it needed to start protecting itself. No bad dreams, no insomnia, and—for a person who has hay fever most months of the year—no allergies, no sneezing at night. Just good old-fashioned hit-the-pillow and pass out.

This night was an exception.

I kept wondering how long will my chemo last, how many will I have, what will they be like.

It's not the pain or the weakness or the hanging around in hospitals I'm worried about. It's the cycling, watching movies in halls, going to the office, wandering around the streets, going to kathak class, skipping off on road trips that I'm thinking about. Things I love.

How am I going to give all of this up?

I slept troubled. When I woke up, the sun was out. And it was just another day. I felt better.

The first thing I had to do was get my mind in shape. My body and I were great friends. We've always been like that. I know it sounds flaky and an 'eat kale, love koalas' type of thing to say, but it's true. I love yoga, because I can stare at my toes or look closely at my knees. I've always felt very comfortable in my own skin. Not in a 'drink green tea and light a candle' way, but in a 'happy to have knobby knees and flat feet' way.

It was my mind I was worried about. Like I said, we were having issues, it just wouldn't let me off the hook. Which is why it was important that I took control and decided how I'll face this. Ahem, I can hear all my friends muttering 'control freak' under their breath.

There were two paths I could take from here. One was fight. Just go in with all guns blazing, muster up every bit of my fighting spirit, call cancer a bastard, grit my teeth at the chemo. Get angry, trash talk, and win this battle.

But my heart wasn't in it. How could I be angry and call this a battle when I kept feeling that the cancer had come to teach me some valuable lessons? And it would go in peace, and not in anger.

There was only one option actually. Which was to become a turtle.

Okay, this is my patented theory. It's also probably the only one I will ever have if I become a god-woman. It involves letting your body go into survival mode. You tuck your head in, wear a shell over your body. That shell doesn't feel anything, and you retreat far into yourself, just mentally withdrawing while you are doing everything needed. Watch what's making you uncomfortable, but don't let it bother you. Slowly, your skeletal body will start to run on autopilot, while every cell of your body is conserving energy.

The other thing I felt is I'm not alone in this. The universe will help me if I ask. My relationship with religion is one of bemused tolerance. And I can't get myself to believe in idol worship. Yet, there are places or things that make me feel like they carry something, something calming and healing. But the thing that I feel closest to in terms of God, is nature.

That morning, I sat on the windowsill of my bedroom and looked out at the tall palm tree leaning towards my window. And the scraggly but filled-with-birds gulmohar next to it. There's a nest in the gulmohar tree. I spot it for the first time that morning. There are two kites hovering around.

I feel it's a sign. These are guys who'll help me. The birds, the trees, the clouds, the sun. I have to call on them to give me strength and heal me. I immediately feel better.

Next is coming to terms with what the oncologist is serving up. I'm weighing it, letting it sit in my head, getting a feel of it.

What are you scared of?

The chemotherapy. And the doctor said there'll be many rounds to it.

That's why it's called therapy, right. And not a chemo shot.

Why are they doing this to me?

Because they have to play safe. They need to carpet bomb your insides, just in case there's some stray cell that's escaped. How can you refuse that? Put on your big girl panties. If there was any chance of cancer being in your body, would you not want it out?

Bloody hell, of course I would.

Then tell the doctor to bring on the SWAT Team and do this.

That's it. Decision made. I would worry about how I'd deal with the chemotherapy when I came to it. For now, I would accept the protocol (ooh, I was getting savvy with the terminology), and I would help myself.

Number one on the help-myself list was yoga. I was going to yoga the ass out of cancer. So, I called Tanvi, who had taught me on and off. I have no idea why I thought of her, and not my other yoga teachers. Maybe because she was gentle and sweet. Or maybe because the universe wanted her to point me to Nupur.

I call Tanvi, and I tell her my diagnoses, and ask her if she can help me with yoga through chemotherapy. And Tanvi tells me, 'Listen baba, first thing you have to do is meet my student Nupur, who recovered from breast cancer two years back.'

I'm grinning my head off, 'She had cancer? And now she's all okay and doing yoga?'

'Ya baba, totally. And she's been practising like a pro now, plus she's a wonderful person to talk to.'

I take Nupur's number, and caution myself. Don't get too excited, what if she's this negative person who totally freaks me out? Then I realize, hell, how can I be more freaked out than I already am?

I call her. She sounds calm, there are no hysterics, and since she lives close by, she suggests meeting up. In a park near the sea, which is close to both our houses. I call Ziba and tell her. Ziba, who knows exactly how flaky I am, says she'd like to come along. I am relieved. Either I'll forget to ask the correct questions or I'll forget the answers. Ziba, I have no doubt, will handle this like a pro.

Number two on the list, the two sets of parents. Like I said, my in-laws live above us, and are blissfully unaware of all the chaos brewing a floor below. Anirban and I decide we don't need to tell them anything for now, or till the surgery is done. They're old, it'll devastate them. Just hearing the C word will freak them out, and

Ma will not sleep nights thinking about who put an evil eye hex on her daughter-in-law.

Then there are my parents. By now they've heard all the scariest things about chemotherapy. Every day, when I call to update them, I can hear the struggle in their voice, and the heartbreak. They want to be here, next to me. But I'm holding them back. I want to process things on my own first, before they arrive. I'm scared their heartbreak and grief will sweep me away, and I'll not be able to see them like that.

But I'm also feeling very guilty about keeping them away.

Anirban and I talk. We decide my parents will have to come for my surgery. I want them, so they can see me, and not be miles away crying and worrying themselves to sleep. But where do they stay? We have a typical Mumbai problem. A 1BHK. Where will my parents sleep? After the surgery I will need the bedroom, and there's no way I want my parents to be sleeping on mattresses on the floor. There's only one way out. We call Koeli didi in Hyderabad. She will need to come down just before my surgery and take my in-laws with her. So, when my parents land, they can stay upstairs. We'll have to plan this perfectly, so there is no overlap.

Third thing on the list is a haircut. I decide there's no point in keeping my long hair. The chemotherapy is going to make it fall off, so I better start getting used to short hair. Really, I have the best plans. But the problem is, cancer has other plans. And nothing could have prepared me for losing my hair.

So off I go, and chop my hair off, and donate it to make wigs for cancer patients. Slight inception feels here. I wonder what if I go to buy a wig, and it turns out to be my own hair. Fuck!

But the short hair is liberating. I look chic and petite and very French. I don't know about you, but in my head I'm not graceful and dainty at all. But with this new short hair, all I want to do is sit in a café, and hold a cup of tea with slim, manicured hands while wearing oversized sunglasses.

But I can't do that. I have a whole job list to go through. And the next thing on it is meeting my dentist. I'm worried that during the chemos I might not be able to continue my treatment as often, so I want to discuss the options.

Oinx comes with me to the dentist. By now, I usually have a chaperone wherever I go. Oinx, Ziba, and Anirban have taken to coordinating with each other, so I'm not alone. It feels a bit like a picnic where I am the chief guest!

We sit in the dentist's waiting room. After ten minutes he comes out and pulls a chair and sits right in front of me. He looks into my eyes and murmurs something. I can't hear him, and I don't want to be rude and say 'Hain?' when he's looking into my eyes with the most pained expression on his face.

He's asking me something. I strain my ears.

'How are you doing?' he murmurs

Damn, can't hear you. Why are you whispering?

'Tell me, are you okay?'

Oh, he's asking if I'm okay. I was fine till you made me feel like I'm going deaf. Just speak up, man.

'Is there anything I can do to help?'

Yes, speak to me like a normal human being.

This was just the start of it. I realized that in the course of my treatment, people often spoke to me in what I started to term was the 'No More Tears, Pushpa' voice. No offence to Pushpa. But they'd speak to me like I was dying, as though if they raised their voice, I'll just crumble and fall to pieces.

Then there were the folks who spoke to me in that 'Extra Happy Person' voice. Punch me in the shoulder and say, 'Yaar, you're a strong girl, you'll beat cancer's ass.'

Really? How do you know? You have a hotline to my oncologist?

Anyway, I console the dentist. By now I'm an expert at consoling people, even though I'm rolling my eyes hysterically in my head. I have a bedside manner that consists of an enigmatic half-smile. People don't want me to be normal. Not my close friends and family, but everyone else. They want some reaction, either I should be hysterical or I should be the strong but suffering Mother India type. Wiping a stray tear with the pallu of my sari before anyone can see it roll down my cheek.

Fine, I'll give it to them.

And the last thing on my list is to see my friends, the alternative flower remedy doctors who helped me during my panic attacks. I reached out to them as soon as I was diagnosed.

In the meantime, I was still getting at least three calls a day from friends, acquaintances, random friends' friends, telling me to go see various alternate doctors. From Dharamshala to Lower Parel. And I was like sorry, I have a million chores to finish, I can't be haring off to Dharamshala or Parel. But I did want to see my flower remedy doctors, who had helped with my anxiety attacks. I knew and trusted them. When I met them with my reports, they were cheerful and said your oncologist is doing the right thing. Which was perfect. The last thing I wanted was confusion. To have an alternate doctor diss your oncologist is a recipe for disaster. They also promised to use flower remedies to build my resistance to the surgery. To help me heal fast. I was thrilled. But, they asked me to meet a metal doctor before that.

What's a metal doctor? Can I only call on him during Black Sabbath? Sorry, some jokes should be allowed in my head, right?

Apparently, your body consists of various metals. Don't ask me the details, because I have no idea. I always thought it consists of water, and the rest is cellulite. But no, there are metals in your body. And sometimes they go out of whack, causing a wobble in the equilibrium and thereby resulting in diseases as well. They gave me the name and number of a person in a far-flung suburb of Mumbai, who I must meet.

I'm in two minds. The person I must meet is my plastic surgeon, and then the anaesthetist. I decide if I have the time, I'll meet the metal detector, sorry doctor, after that.

The next day, I'm back at Kokilaben, with Anirban at my side. We're getting smarter at hospital hacks and we have the first appointment of the day at 9 a.m. Which also shows you how early doctors start their day. I struggle to get to work by 11 a.m., so I'm always mighty impressed with how doctors start their day so early.

It's 8.45 and we're waiting. There are three metal chairs, joined together, in a long corridor. We're sitting there. The same chairs are spaced out all along the corridor. It's empty and silent. There are no windows, no natural light, just the white antiseptic glare of the tube lights above. I can see the light bounce off the tiled floor and walls. It looks like something is about to happen. Maybe a flood of blood is going to come cascading down the corridors. This is a great setting for a horror movie.

Just then, I smell a gust of aftershave. And look up to see a well-dressed, dapper man walk into one of the rooms. That's the room I'm supposed to walk into. That's the man who is going to make me a new boob.

I, by the way, have now stalked Dr Mandar and Dr Quazi on every platform I can find. My logic is simple. If you're going to be making yourself so familiar with my boobs, then I better make myself familiar with you.

I like the fact that they have both worked at Tata Memorial. It's like having Jai and Veeru take care of me. Plus, it's good to know both your surgeons know each other and have probably done this together many times. It's like your tailor, the guy who's measuring you and noting it down on that little bill book, and the guy who's going to decipher those scrawled measurements and actually stitch the garment—it's best if they have worked together, and know each other's coded drawings.

We get called into Dr Quazi's room. It's bare, but he's smiling at me. I immediately like him. I show him my file and tell him that Dr Mandar asked me to see him. He asks me when the operation is scheduled for. I stare at him and tell him I have no idea. I guess they are going to decide that based on what he says. He laughs, tells me to go to the examining table, and calls for a nurse.

Now I've become smart. I carry my backpack to the examination table and slip my bra in. Pro move! He comes, feels the breast, makes me stand. And then checks my stomach, sides and back. He smiles and says, 'I see you are very fit, but that's a problem for us. I have no fat that I can take from your stomach.'

I want to hug him and do a dance.

And I also want to sigh and curse my blasted luck. Here I am, in the best shape I ever was, not an ounce of extra fat, flat stomach, and guess what … I have cancer. Damn.

'So we'll take the tissue from here.' And he taps at my left shoulder blade. And we'll take a graft of skin from here as well.'

My eyes widen. He says he'll explain everything. But his worry is the tattoo on my left shoulder. It's a beautiful tattoo of vines and leaves and it says 'pick the present' in French. Not because I know French, but because the tattoo artist was French. And I just wanted it in a different language.

He frowns and looks at my back and finally he's satisfied. 'We can save the tattoo. If it had been a little lower it would have been a problem, but this is manageable.'

How sweet. I realize then that plastic surgeons are really nice. They accept all your vanities and don't judge at all. In fact, their job is to make you look even nicer. Imagine, a surgeon worrying about sacrificing my tattoo.

I take the chance to put across an alternate solution. Maybe, he could take some tissue off my hips, or my bum. How about that? I go in for a mastectomy and come out looking all svelte and slim-hipped.

Is slim-hipped even a word? It should be. I mean, I dream of being slim-hipped all the time. It's the unattainable body of the women in Gap ads who have really long legs and very narrow hips, and look stunningly athletic and yet girly in their jeans.

Jeans have been my nemesis for years. I love them, but shopping for them exposes the wonderfully complicated relationship between my hip and waist. If they fit around the waist, they'll never go up my hips. And if they fit around the hips, then the waist is so loose that I have to wear a belt and look like Pooja Bhatt from the 80s. Plus, the length. No, I don't have long legs, and you can make a whole other garment from the amount you have left after resizing my denims.

So, I slyly slip in the offer to take my hip or bum fat. But I'm guessing the doctor has heard that one before, because he grins and shakes his head.

Fine.

I dress and go back to the chair. He's writing something out. I realize it's my surgery plan, and as part of it he's made the standard boob drawing.

Except there is nothing standard about it. That's when I realize every doctor has his or her signature style of drawing boobs. They are no way representational of the actual stuff on your chest. Some do a stick figure kind of drawing, and that is the most basic version. Like my gyneac. She just made some long and tired-looking boobs.

The first oncologist drew them in a hurried textbook fashion. And then there are those who make them with the practised flourish of an artist leaving his signature style across the prescription pad. I like those doctors. Like my onco surgeon drew them brilliantly. Perfect shape, size, everything. And the plastic surgeon, same. Modestly Blaise kind of sharp boobs.

There's a lovely Urdu word for it. For signature style, not the drawing of boobs!

It's called takeeya kalam.

I looked at Dr Quazi's takeeya kalam boob drawing, and I knew he was the right person for me.

Of course, the doctor had no idea that I was impressed with his artistic skills. He was outlining what was going to happen to me. He was going to take tissue from my back. There would be a scar there. And some skin would be grafted from my back to create a patch where my nipple was. The body, as usual being all awesome and amazing, would grow back that skin on the back.

They would create a channel from my back to the left breast and fill it with tissue, and then stitch it back up like a cushion cover. Since it was my own tissue, there was no worry about the body rejecting it. Also, if I put on weight, the boob would grow like the other one, and if I lost weight both would shrink.

Damn, I already have small boobs, how much more will they shrink?

In fact, my crazy cousins in the family WhatsApp group are urging me to get the doctor to give me bigger boobs. We all have the same body type. Small till the waist. And then a big Mukherjee bum!

Till now, everything sounds easy-peasy. Then the surgeon adds a however.

However, there will be tubes attached to me for the first couple of days. These tubes will drain out the excess tissue. And I will need to keep coming back to the hospital, once my tubes are removed, so they can keep draining the tissue.

The recovery will take longer. Because it's not just a mastectomy. It's also stitching, grafting, building pipelines and drains across my back. And the surgery will be long. At least three hours. Which makes it a five-hour surgery in total.

I'm not worried about the time. I'll be out cold, under anaesthesia. It's not like oh, five hours of just lying there with my eyes open, and no Kindle with me.

What I'm feeling reluctant about is the extra days in the hospital. I would like to get out as soon as possible. I don't really have the fondest memories of hospitals. And these pipes will just tie me back.

The surgeon is looking at me. I have to say okay.

I take a deep breath. It's now or never. If I don't do the reconstruction now, it can only be done two years later. Don't ask me why, I didn't ask. And most importantly, they will not have the flap of my breast. Because that will of course be discarded and my chest will just be stitched up where the breast was.

This is the easiest way to do it.

Unless I ask them to save the flap.

And where will you keep it? In your wallet?

Ughhh. No.

I nod at Dr Quazi. I'm getting my breast reconstruction done.

He beams at me. I feel a sense of déjà vu. And he tells me that it'll be perfect. My left breast will look exactly like my right breast. In my head I'm thinking, 'Right. You're forgetting that the only difference is this breast will not have a nipple.'

There's no time to brood over that, because he's picked up the phone and called Dr Mandar, and told him that it's a go. He puts down the phone and tells us we need to quickly see Dr Mandar. So, after our thank yous, off we go to the cancer department.

This time there's no waiting. The doctor is all business, and he says, 'Great, you have to meet the anaesthetist and get some tests done, and let's do the surgery on Monday.'

Whaaaaatttttt.

This is Friday.

A life-changing surgery in three days. What about prep time? Like you know, mentally prepare myself time?

He looks at my face and says, 'There's nothing to think about. Let's get this out as soon as possible.'

Which is correct. But I've gone into brain freeze mode. And am just grinning and nodding and even saying 'yay' when he says let's get this out. I mean, which patient who is going to have a major surgery says 'Yay' to her onco? I see Anirban looking at me, he knows that I'm flaky.

Lucky for me, he's not flaky. So, he asks all the correct questions.

The operation will take five hours. Mandy will do his thing, and scrape out the breast. For some reason I keep picturing him with a coconut scraper. And then Dr Quazi will swoop in and fill it with my tissue and pat it into place like he's making samosas. I have no idea why I keep seeing these food parallels, but one thing is for sure, they make it easier to digest what's going to happen. See what I did there!

Then he tells us about the most important thing. Which at that time because of my 'I am so gobsmacked that I can't process anything' state, I barely registered. While he operates on me, he will insert something called a port on my right side, at the start of my chest. It'll go just under my skin, and be connected to my jugular vein.

Jugular vein? Is that what he said?

Yes. The one they cut in the whodunits.

Holy fuck! How will I live if he's going to be cutting into my jugular vein?

But I say nothing. Just smile my ass off.

He continues to tell us that instead of sticking needles into my vein, and letting the chemo go through my hand, the chemo will be injected through the port and then through the jugular it'll get distributed all over.

It still doesn't register, and it's only later that I realize Mandy has taken the best decision on my behalf.

We leave his room. Our panic has just skyrocketed.

We have time to meet the anaesthetic. So, we pop into the Starbucks downstairs. This is why they have a coffee shop in the hospital. So patients like me can stress eat. I order the sweetest thing possible, it's good for shock!

Anirban's friends, who I also know, have popped in to see me. They've heard the news and just want to say hi, especially since they live close by.

And it's odd. I don't know how to be. I don't want to talk about my feelings, or the fact that I have surgery in three days. Neither can I talk about normal stuff like which show are you watching. That just seems bizarre. So, what do I say?

My whole life is changing in front of my eyes, and I can't talk. I know they're being nice, and they've come to see me. But I feel like a specimen in a Petri dish.

It's a short meeting. I mean, how long will you hang out in a hospital? They hug me and wish me luck, and leave. And I think of them stepping into the warm sun, walking home, making plans for the evening, just normal things on a Friday evening. And I will have none of that. I feel jealous. I also feel mean, but I can't help it. It just sucks that I can't be the one walking out into the sun, without a care in the world.

20

By the time we get back home, it's evening and I am starting to panic. I only have the weekend. When will my parents get here, when will we send my in-laws, when will I meet the cancer survivor lady Nupur, the one my yoga teacher had put me in touch with?

We decide to walk across to a café right next to our house. Oinx, who has quit her current job and is looking forward to a break, is also back from work. She bursts in to tell me that her notice period is ending, and she'll be able to spend all her time with me when I'm going through surgery and chemo.

'But aren't you going to Scotland for a holiday?'

'I cancelled it!'

She had planned this for two months, and I know she was looking forward to it. And yet she's standing there, grinning her head off, telling me she cancelled it.

I want to cry. Because I feel so loved. And because she's had to cancel this trip.

She brushes off my protests, with a 'Stop being so emo. Tell me what Mandy said'.

As we fill her in, I start to panic again. I can't have this surgery on Monday. Mandy has told me all surgeries happen on Mondays, Wednesdays, and Fridays. And he's also given me his number. I'm going to muster up some courage and call him.

The call gets forwarded.

'Hi Doctor, this is Shormistha.'

'Tell me?'

'Doctor, I just wanted to know if I could push my surgery to Wednesday from Monday.'

'Why? Astrologer told you?'

Whaaaat?

'No, no, I just have a lot of things to do before that.'

'Okay. We'll do it on Wednesday.'

Whew. That's sorted. I'm so relieved, I wolf down some mutton rolls, and make a list of everything I have to do. Only to realize Anirban and Oinx are grinning. They've already made a list.

Ziba is in charge. New bedsheets and covers. Sanitizers. Gloves. Tissue paper. There's a list of post-operative stuff that needs to be bought, to make the house patient-proof and infection-proof.

Fine. I get down to the other stuff. Starting with the money. I ask my insurance agent what kind of room I am entitled to. He checks and says with my Mediclaim, I can take any room I want. I am so excited. I tell Anirban. He's the one who will go to the hospital a day before and complete all the formalities.

Next, I have to meet Nupur, the breast cancer survivor.

Ziba and I arrive at Jogger's Park at 5 p.m. the next day. It's a beautiful balmy evening. We find Nupur on one of the benches facing the sea. She's a petite woman with shoulder length hair and a very calm but determined air about her. I introduce myself and thank her for meeting us.

She asks me about my diagnosis, and then I ask about hers. She tells me she was treated in Delhi by a fantastic doctor, and she's still very much in touch with Dr Rohatgi. I nod.

Ziba suddenly turns and shakes me by the shoulder. Her eyes are shining.

'She said Rohatgi!'

Just to give you context, I am terrible with names. I believe I have other things to store in my brain, and names are not one of them. And so, I remember people by an approximate name. If your name is Sushil, I'll remember you as Charles.

That doesn't bode very well for me when I spot someone and yell out to them on the street. They never turn.

So while I'm nodding away, Ziba suddenly shakes me. Her eyes are shining.

'She said Rohatgi!'

I look at Ziba blankly. She is exasperated. 'Isn't he the doctor you spoke to in Delhi? The one Tarini put you in touch with, who said you should go to Kokilaben if they are moving faster?'

Oh my god. Yes. And he's the guy who treated Nupur. Nupur is also all smiles. It's an icebreaker, and also, another sign. I look at Nupur while she talks to me, and I feel calm. I know that I've found myself a guide who has been there, done that, and who'll gently navigate me through troubled waters.

Nupur tells me things that set the tone for our friendship, and also how I'll prepare myself mentally. She tells me that the most important thing is to listen to my body. And to put myself at the centre of everything. While my strong support system will back me, it's my body and my mind that are going to hell and back. So, I'm going to need to make sure I am in a state of calm.

I tell her that I read somewhere that cancer cells feed on drama, on high emotion, on unhappiness. She agrees, and tells me that's why it's necessary to avoid anything that might upset me or throw me off.

There should be no space for ups and downs, and I must stay balanced emotionally to allow my body to heal and my mind to support it.

For all my flakiness, it registers. I've been so lost and sad for the last year or more, that I have to release it. I have to let it go, that's my path to getting well.

We sit in the park, looking out into the sea. She tells me how she moved to Rishikesh during her chemo. Because she wanted to be close to nature. It was hard, her husband, kids, parents, in-laws, everyone moved. But she was sure that being surrounded by mountains would help her heal. I listen, quietly, amazed at her determination to listen to herself. That's what I must do.

I need to stop thinking about others, who will feel bad, who will not. I need to be ready to draw a line, and politely say no when I want to.

I'm also very happy to hear about Nupur's love for nature. I tell her how I've been thinking that the sea, birds, trees, clouds, wind will heal me. She doesn't laugh or look at me blankly. She just nods and says, 'They will.'

I leave the park that evening feeling many kilos lighter. I know I can do this. Nupur has been put in my path to guide me. What also thrills me is that she's a geek. A computer engineer who's obviously super good at what she does, she takes research to the next level.

She tells me that juicing really worked for her. I nod. I've read a little about it. Then she goes on to tell me about a masticating juicer. Apparently, there are two kinds of juicers, and this one is better because it chews through the fruit and extracts the juice. My mind is blown.

Nupur has also done research on ice caps. Not the global warming kinds, but the kind that prevent hair fall during chemo. Basically, you keep wearing an ice cap on your head through your chemo sessions, and it freezes your hair follicles, so they don't fall.

I can't imagine doing so much. I would do anything for my hair not to fall. But I'm also very lazy, not just to do the actual wearing, but even to comprehend how it works. I'm the kind of person who buys Ikea furniture and gives up trying to assemble it in five minutes. Plus, I worry my sinus will kill me if I put ice caps on my head.

But Nupur's geekiness means she's already researched every single thing, and I just have it on a platter.

The next thing for me to do is tell Mom and Dad to come. The minute we call Koeli didi and tell her my surgery date, she books a flight for the weekend. She's coming to take my in-laws to her place in Hyderabad. They still have no idea, and I feel wretched telling them things like I cut my hair because it's too hot. It breaks my heart because they love my new haircut. They are also excited about going on a holiday, though they're wondering what the rush is. We book them on a 12 p.m. flight from Mumbai to Hyderabad, a day before my surgery. And then I call my folks. I break the news of the surgery date. Mom and Dad are ready, their bags are packed. I book them on a 12 p.m. flight from Delhi to Mumbai. Both sets of parents will be flying out at the same time.

I feel bad, the trouble everyone is taking, suspending their lives for me. And the money being spent. But I tell myself, there's no place for guilt, there's only place for healing. Put it aside, and focus on yourself. And let everyone focus on you.

Anirban is getting everything organized like a pro. He's the one who is executing these plans, getting things for the house, reassuring my parents, coordinating with my chief cheerleaders Oinx and Ziba. He's bought enough sanitizer for me to bathe in it. I watch him throw himself into making sure everything is set up for me, and I see shadows under his eyes. I know he's scared, and I know he's realizing, just like me, that we drifted so far away. That we've grown up together, and now to think that we would have lost each other, is just unbearable. He never says he's scared, but he holds me a lot.

I take myself off the WhatsApp group that updates everyone on my diagnoses and protocol. I realize my friends also need a place where they can express how worried they are.

My next task is the metal doctor. I take Oinx along with me. She's always game for any mad idea I might have. We land up in this far-flung suburb and start looking for the address. Turns out the metal doctor is actually a dentist. Or maybe he's not, and he just has a dentist's chair in the room.

He's this lanky guy in jeans, who's sitting in a corner shop in a small community shopping centre. There's a table next to the dentist's chair, and in the distance, there are two female attendants who are fanning themselves. It's a bizarre scene from a David Dhawan movie. I tell him a little about myself. He says he charges ₹4,000 to do a metal test. I say okay. Even though in my head I'm thinking, 'Not okay.'

He starts to explain how there are metals present in our bodies, and if there's too much or too little of a particular metal, then the body is susceptible to illness. He then tells me to put my hand on a mouse-like device which is connected to his laptop, and that apparently will read and gauge the metal toxicity in my body. I'm not sure about this, but I've already given him the money. So, I sit there with my hand on the mouse thinking, I can't believe I am doing this.

Of course, the results, when they arrive on his laptop ten minutes later, state that all my metal levels are wrong, and there's serious imbalance happening.

No shit, Sherlock, I got breast cancer, even I can tell you there is imbalance happening!

Anyway, I patiently listen to him, and so does Oinx, who is taking copious notes on her phone. I love her for the fact that when it comes to my health, and me getting better, she'll take anything seriously. Including this man who is now telling us how he takes injections that boost the metals in his body and how I can even take a genetic test for it. Only, it costs an arm and a leg.

Thanks, but no thanks. Already going to be missing a breast, not so keen to part with other limbs.

What finally gets us to run from the place is when he starts to talk about his digestion. He says he has the worst gut bacteria ever. And his wife has a cast iron stomach, great digestion, great motions. Oinx and I are now fidgeting in our seats. Do we really want to know about his wife's bowels? But no, he continues. And he tells us how he sorted this out by doing a faecal transplant.

There's a moment of silence while we try to comprehend if we heard this wrong.

Apparently not. He took his wife's potty and had it transplanted into his gut, so his gut could have her good bacteria.

I know in a marriage it's good to share everything, but this is going too far. Both Oinx and I manage to smile as he describes the details. But the minute he pauses, we jump in saying we're late and run.

On the way back, my belief that I have to make my peace with allopathy is strengthened. There'll be many people who will recommend many healers, babas, people who read your pulse, your metal toxicity, your horoscope, your navel, but the only one I can rely on at this moment, without batting an eyelid or spending a mini fortune on, is my onco surgeon.

Saturday, Sunday, and Monday whizz by. My aunt decides to come for a night to see me. She's flown down from the US for some other work, but manages a detour. I tell her we have to go for sushi, because I have to eat all the things I love before chemotherapy.

Of course, this is Mumbai. Where on a Saturday night it's impossible to get a table in a good sushi place. So finally, in exasperation, I call back the place that said they were full, and tell them I have breast cancer and I have surgery on Wednesday, and surely they can't refuse me a reservation. There's a long pause on the other end. I can almost hear the person's brain ticking, wondering if this is a horribly ghoulish prank or not. Finally, he plays safe, and gives me a table. Actually, the best table in the house.

That evening, I also ask my whole office to come and meet me in a pub near my house. I know they're all worried, or generally just wondering how it's going. And people are not used to not having me around in office, so there must be a lot of uncertainty. Plus, they all want to wish me luck, and I don't know how many days it would be before I see them again. So, I drop into the pub in the afternoon, and tell them I have breast cancer, and my surgery is in two days, so can I please get a reservation. I get the best two tables, in a pub where there are only three tables!

The last place I need to use this sympathy card is with the waxing lady.

Waxing before a surgery?! Seriously?

Ha, I can tell this is what you're thinking.

But this is no ordinary waxing. I have heard that before a big surgery happens, the nurses come and shave people completely. And when I say completely, I mean completely. I am guessing doctors do not want you lying naked there, with tufts of short, curly hair staring them in the face.

Fine, if they want a freshly plucked chicken, they will get that. But I was not going to take a chance, and let any nurse come near my hoo-ha with a razor blade. I would get a Brazilian wax, even if it killed me, before I let that happen.

So, I called the waxing lady at the fancy salon near my house. This lady by the way is far busier than a CEO of any Fortune 500 company. And, of course, she has no time for this urgent request for waxing. Till I drop my voice a couple of notches and whisper in my most 'bechari ladki' voice, 'I've been diagnosed with breast cancer, and have surgery on Wednesday.' Ta-da! Waxing appointment is booked.

Before I know it, it's Tuesday morning. My parents are settled upstairs. Okay, I use the word 'settled' loosely. They are most unsettled, they're sad, worried out of their minds, and tomorrow their only daughter is going to have a five-hour surgery. And that's just the start of her treatment.

What makes matters slightly difficult is the only daughter is going about behaving like it's all perfectly normal. And that makes them think that I'm being brave and hiding my pain.

When I look back, I think that's a mistake I made. I didn't give Mom and Dad a chance to let stuff sink in. To come to the hospital a couple of times, to meet my oncologist, to talk to me about how I was feeling, to talk about how they were feeling.

I had already accepted everything, and gone beyond that stage of being unsure. I was relaxed and calm. I was ten steps ahead of them, and it never struck me that I should slow down. But then, at that time, you do what you feel is correct. And there's no manual to go by. Yes, in retrospect, I feel it would have made the initial weeks and months easier for them, and me.

Tuesday morning, the day I have to leave for the hospital, feels like a long day. There's a sense of not being able to do anything. Like being suspended in limbo. Anirban went to the hospital a day earlier, to complete the insurance formalities. It takes ages and ages. Hospitals and insurance companies are frenemies. Can't live without each other, or with each other. But he comes back with a big smile. I am a genius, my health insurance has come through, and he's managed to get me a VIP room.

I am super excited. My middle-class sensibilities are cautioning me. I check with him a hundred times if it's totally covered. Will we get a rude shock later? Did you ask about hidden charges? Did you double- and triple-check, and then check again?

He's confident, shows me the admission form. I wonder if I should pack my best clothes. But finally settle for the same clothes I've worn to every hospital visit. They are turning out to be my security blanket. I pack my bag, add my Kindle, a new lip balm and my earphones.

I manage to take a quick walk in my lane. Just to stare at the trees and the sunshine. I wonder when I'll walk down this lane again.

Lunch is a subdued affair. Anirban's gone to the hospital to submit some papers for the insurance. Mom and Dad are obviously very stressed. Poor things, they just landed yesterday, and now it's time to go to the hospital, and tomorrow is my surgery. They barely eat anything.

I can't wait to go. It's like an exam. I'm just sick of the build-up. I want to get there and just finish it off.

At 5 p.m., when I am just about bouncing off the walls, we leave. Ziba is coming to drop me, along with my parents and Anirban. She slips a small statue of Mother Mary in my bag.

I grin at her. Yet another sign. Like I said, I'm not religious. But I believe in energy or vibes or whatever you call it. And one of those places is Mount Mary, close to where I live. There's a church and a statue of Mother Mary facing the sea. When you sit or stand there, the first thing you notice is there are people from every religion, every walk of life there. The next thing you notice will be how the sun warms your shoulders, and the faintest sea breeze ruffles your hair, telling you it'll be okay.

I decide this statue will go everywhere with me, through my treatment.

21
ω

You know that railway station feeling? Where lots of people have come to see you off. But the train is delayed. And now they are waiting, and so are you. And all the jokes and hugging are done. And gradually everyone is feeling tired and hungry. And you're constantly looking up and down the platform, waiting for the announcement, feeling bad that everyone is just hanging around for you.

Take that feeling, and add lots of worry and stress to it.

That's how it felt.

We were all in the lobby of the hospital. Ziba was going to go back with Mom and Dad. And Anirban was going to stay the night with me.

In spite of Anirban having come in and done everything earlier, there were still loads of forms to fill, and the admission process was taking ages. I went to the canteen with Mom, Dad, and Ziba. Note, not Starbucks, because parents would have not even breathed the air there once they saw the price of tea and coffee. If you want your parents to eat something, take them to a canteen. When they see steel ka cups and thali, and plastic chairs, they feel reassured.

They weren't hungry. But we managed to have a dosa and make some stilted conversation. Told you about that railway station feeling, right? Finally, at about 7.30 p.m., all the paperwork was done. We still didn't know what time the surgery was, though.

I hugged Mom and Dad. I didn't want to see them cry. I wanted to just focus on staying calm and cheerful. Anirban and I gently told them that as soon as we hear about the surgery time, we'll tell them. I also convinced them that they don't need to come and sit in the hospital all morning, and through the whole five-hour surgery. I don't know if they heard me. All I could see was pain in their eyes.

Ziba hugged me, and they were gone. Mom kept turning around and looking at me. I made myself walk away.

I have one weakness, and that's not being able to handle my parents being sad. I had to stay focused.

I walk to the lift with Anirban, he's holding my hand. 'It's a special lift that goes all the way to the sixteenth floor, which is where you are.'

I grin at him as we ride up, in our fancy elevator.

We get off, and it is like a hotel floor. Massive corridor, beautiful coffee shop-like table and chairs laid out, a big nurses' reception humming with efficiency, and right at the end, a massive door.

Not just any door, but a rich person's door. I'll tell you what that is. It's a door that you have to put all your weight onto to push open. Not our normal, flimsy doors with their latches. These are solid fellows, and you certainly can't put a grill door before them.

In fact, my theory is that rich people even have furniture like that. I remember going to a Bollywood superstar's house once to take him through an ad film script, and it took me ten minutes to wrestle with his personal lift door and then another ten minutes to move the dining table chair so I could clamber on.

Anyway, once we heave open the rich person's door, there's a room the size of my flat! I could have asked my parents and all my friends to move in there. It's a huge football field, with a hospital bed in the

centre of it, and a sofa near the windows. It has a massive attached
bath. And next to it, is a smaller room, done up hotel-style. Thick
mattress, warm lamps, dressing table, and another attached bathroom.
The patient's area has tube lights and the caregiver area has lovely
yellow lighting. I consider taking one of the lamps and putting it on
the metal table beside my bed, but decide against it. I am just too
excited. To me, this is the lifestyle of the rich and famous.

A nurse comes in and gives me clothes to change into. I wander
into the massive bathroom and for a second, I'm seized with this,
'damn, this is so nice, but I'll hardly be able to enjoy it' feeling. I shake
it off, slip into the pyjama and shirt handed to me. This set is yellow
with tiny flowers on it, and the shirt doesn't have a collar. I look in
the mirror and decide it's really not doing anything for me. I look like
an old Chinese lady who sells momos at Kolkata's Chinatown. Solid
colours would have worked far better.

Anyway, they strap a band on my wrist with my name, etc. I ask
them when the surgery is, and the nurse says they'll let me know in
a while. She leaves. I jump on to my hospital bed. It's comfy and it
can be moved up and down, but I wonder why it's so narrow. Thank
god they have railings on the sides, or I'd fall off every time I turn.

The rest is routine. Sending photos to my parents and friends,
keeping my things, arranging my Kindle and the Mother Mary
statue on the table next to my bed, figuring out where the lights are,
dinner arriving, opening it to realize, yes, this is a hospital. And the
food sucks. Really, I feel like they get the guys who fail the Railway
Catering exam to cook in hospitals. There's black custard with my
meal. I mean, who on earth has heard of black custard? It sort of
defeats the purpose of having a sunny, happy dessert like a custard,
doesn't it?

I eat some of the dinner. I'm beginning to feel wound up now.
Anirban's gone down. A friend of ours had a heart attack, and he's in

the same hospital. A lot of our acquaintances are downstairs in the lobby. Anirban is meeting some of them.

I call my parents. I keep imagining them sitting alone, barely eating anything, and I want to reach out and hug them. And yet, when I call and they sound worried, I want to put the phone down. I just can't handle it.

Half an hour later, a young doctor walks in. She checks the tag on my wrist, asks if I'm okay, and tells me my surgery is scheduled for 3 p.m. tomorrow.

Three p.m.???? Damn, I have to wait suspended in this going-to-be-operated-on state till then. I wanted my surgery to be early in the morning. So it's over. And the doctors are fresh. By 3 p.m., they'll be bored of cutting up people. I try asking the young doctor if my surgery can be moved up, without giving her these reasons obviously. But no luck.

The nurses come back. I can't eat or drink anything after midnight, they tell me. As soon as they leave, I grab the rest of my dinner and black custard and polish it off. My problem is the minute someone tells me you can't eat or drink for a couple of hours, just then I'll feel hungry or thirsty. Like going to the loo. If you tell me there's no loo for a couple of hours, my bladder will overhear the conversation, and the next minute, I'll be dying to pee.

A few minutes later, another nurse walks in. She smiles at me, I smile back. Then very awkwardly she takes out a razor. Ta da!!!!! I don't say anything. She tells me she'll have to shave me in preparation for the surgery. I give her a huge smile and say, already done. She comes close and inspects my arms and legs. And says, 'Okay, but we have to shave everything, so you take off your pyjamas.' I grin and I say, 'EVERYTHING is done' as I whip off my pyjamas and she has a look. I have never seen a happier smile on someone's face. She exclaims, 'No one has ever come prepared like this.' We are both so pleased with the situation. As she's leaving, she tells me, 'Good only, it was my first time with this new razor.' I look at Mother Mary next to me, and silently thank her.

That night, I sleep like a baby. Till at an unearthly hour of 6 a.m., when the nurses start to stream in. I've just gotten cosy and am having nice dreams. It feels like the Mumbai–Delhi Rajdhani. Just when you are snuggled under that railway blanket because the AC has now frozen your nose, and the gentle rocking of the train has put you into this lovely deep sleep, they start blaring the morning news on the speakers, and the attendants start banging a thermos full of tea on to your berth and demanding that you return the blankets now, because Delhi is just another two hours away.

The nurses start an IV, and I'm still trying to sleep. No point staying awake when I can't eat. Anirban is going home to bathe, and get fresh clothes, and bring my parents. I've already told most of my friends not to come for the surgery. It'll only end by 8 p.m. Anirban and I have lied to my parents and said no one is allowed to visit my room before the surgery.

Mom, Dad, I am so sorry about this. Remember that it's not that I didn't want you. It's just that I was in the zone. You know the zone that cricketers or footballers or any sports person talks about, where you only focus on what you have to do. The crowds, the heat, the discomfort—you tune that out. Till there's just silence. I was in that zone. Don't ask me how. Maybe it was the yoga, maybe it was because I felt safe being surrounded by people who loved me, maybe it was because I liked my doctor. Or maybe it's because I knew I had no other choice.

Letting you come there would upset that equilibrium. Even if I had explained this to you, how would you have hidden the worry, the pain? How would you have watched me lie there, waiting? Or the nurses coming in and out? And then your pain would have been the only thing I would notice and worry about. I'm sorry, I know how upset you were, and how much you wanted to see me, but this was the best thing to do, for me.

Oinx came in early, to fill in for Anirban. I could tell that she was worried sick, but keeping a cheerful front. I think of all my friends, Oinx was most affected by what had happened to me. And because she's very emotional, it was harder for her. We didn't talk much. I kept listening to a lot of breathing meditation, and dozing off.

At about 11 a.m., two nurses come in and say they'll take me on a wheelchair to the basement to the nuclear medicine department. They'd inject my breast with a dye, so when they are doing the surgery if anything at all lit up, they could have another look, or take it out.

Oinx comes down with me. I am hungry by now, and I keep telling her I want mutton rolls and biryani. But instead, I get some more injections and I am wheeled upstairs.

Time crawled that day. And then suddenly, everything started happening all at once.

Around 1 p.m., the nurses and a ward boy walk in, they are ready to wheel me out. Oinx is starting to panic at the suddenness, and also because Anirban is still on his way back. I keep looking for a stretcher and realize it's the bed; it has wheels, they are just going to take me in that. Ziba, who has just arrived at the hospital, literally skids into the room as they are taking me out, and shoots some videos! The nurses look a little horrified and so I start to blabber, saying that she's a filmmaker, until I realize that they are not interested.

Off I go, with the bed and all, into a lift. Now I get why the bed is so narrow, it has to fit into the lift!

And then we pass more corridors, and I'm staring at the tube lights on the ceiling, till finally they wheel me into a giant room. It's the pre-surgery line up. I'm calm and actually happy that it's time. The nurse leaves my huge file at the foot of my bed. I look around. From where I'm lying, I can see empty beds. I guess the folks who occupied them are in the OT. I can also tell that there are others who have been wheeled in.

A little distance from me lies an elderly lady. She's sleeping. I can see tubes and pipes connected to her bed. The nurses keep coming and checking on her. One even tries to wake her up. Just then a junior doctor type strolls up to my bed. He picks up my file, looks through it, and says, 'Shormistha? Bengali? Shob bhalo?'

Dude, this is not the time to hit on me. I haven't had a sip of water for over twelve hours, my mouth is crusty and smelly. You do not want me to open it.

I smile weakly and shut my eyes. He takes the hint and goes.

Then I hear some raised voices. There's a doctor and a nurse having it out. She's obviously the strict head nurse, and he's the grumpy senior doctor. Or it looks like that. And the fight has something to do with the elderly lady who hasn't come out of anaesthesia as yet, and how she should not be disturbed. They are now yelling at each other. Their juniors scuttle to different ends of the room, and a junior doctor is now standing right beside my head. I shut my eyes tight.

I have a flashback to the dog bite incident when the plastic surgeon had to stitch up my nose. Now since that was under local anaesthesia, I was awake and watching the junior doctors prepare me. One of them was talking on the phone while absent-mindedly cleaning my nose and eye area. Just then the plastic surgeon strode in. The cleaning liquid was going into my eye, and I tried to remove it. Before I could even blink, the surgeon had walked over, leaned over me, and slapped the careless junior doctor's hand. The junior's phone went clattering across the massive OT. And I was like, oh fuck, please don't have a fist fight here. I can't even run properly because the cleaning liquid has dribbled into my eye.

No dude. I do not want to be called into this fight between the nurse and the doctor as an eyewitness. I have a surgery coming up. I keep my eyes shut. And will the junior doctor move on?

Thankfully, he does. But by then the attendants have arrived to wheel me in.

I'm staring around, I want to remember everything. They wheel me into the first door. Dang! What a disappointment. It is nothing like the OT in *ER* or *Grey's Anatomy*. It's a small, dumpy little room with three operating lights. I wanted drama, and hot surgeons in scrubs flying around the place. No such luck. However, I'm taken in by the timing. They said my operation would be at 3 p.m., and the clock shows exactly that. And I see someone in scrubs write the time on a large whiteboard where all the information of the surgery is detailed out. I'm impressed by the exactness.

I'm wheeled next to an even narrower steel bed, that's all set with a blue sheet. I'm guessing that's the operating table. I clamber on to it, and wonder loudly how patients don't fall off. Everyone in the OT is now busy, there's no time to answer my stupid questions. There's someone opening what looks like a wrapped cutlery set (I'm guessing that's where they keep the knives and stuff), while another person puts a rubber ring under my head (what, no pillow!).

They fix some tubes on me. I ask the anaesthetist, 'Have you given me the anaesthesia?' She smiles and says no.

The assistant surgeon says, 'Don't induce, doctor is on his way.'

The door opens, Mandy walks in. He asks me two questions, 'How are you feeling?' And 'Do you wear plunging necklines?'

What??? Is this a trick question?

I say, 'Sometimes. No, no … not really. But ya … maybe.'

He turns to the anaesthetist and says, 'Okay.' I see her give me the injection. And then there is a feeling, like a warm blanket creeping up on me, from my toes, covering my legs. I say, 'I can feel it, I can feel it …' And that's it … I'm out cold.

22
ധ

Two seconds later, the five-hour-long operation is done. And I hear a voice say, 'Shormistha, wake up, the surgery is over.'

Of course, it wasn't the same for everyone outside. My parents and three of my closest friends—Ziba, Gauri, and Vidhya—were in the lobby of the hospital. The girls took turns to sit with my parents over five long hours. Dad was absolutely silent. Mom was agonizing over why I opted for the reconstruction. She was worried about the length of the operation.

Here's the thing I've noticed. Everyone freaks out thinking the longer the operation, the more serious it is. And, of course, this was a serious operation. They were going to be removing the cancerous cells from my body.

(Dear reader, you have no idea how difficult it is for me to even write these words. For all my acceptance and positivity, it's hard to say the word 'cancer'. Like He Who Must Not Be Named in Harry Potter. In fact, I find myself being able to say breast cancer far more easily than cancer. It's as if the specificity of it makes it less scary to mention. And also, the fact that it's a common cancer, and so by using the words 'breast cancer', I feel a sense of reassurance.)

But back to my point, everyone was getting stressed because of the length. In fact, Anirban and Oinx were in the waiting room, near the OT. And after two and a half hours, they started to freak out, because they expected the onco surgeon to come and tell them his part is done and now the plastic surgeon will be going in. It's the damn movies. We're used to the shot of the tired surgeon walking out, while removing his gloves and saying, 'Patient is doing fine.' People, he's a fake doctor. Don't expect a doctor who has multiple surgeries to do to keep popping his head out to tell you not to worry.

Anyway, I remember coming out of general anaesthesia in a haze. I can hear Anirban's voice as they're telling him the surgery went well, and they'll keep me in the waiting area for a while. I'm trying so hard to blink and tell him I'm all good, but I just can't. It's like your brain is active, but your body is this uncooperative slab of meat.

Anirban is asked to wait in the room. And they're getting ready to take me back there. That's when, in my semi-comatose state, I hear the nurses talking about something that's running out of charge. Another voice says something to the effect of, 'Let's take her up quickly before it runs out of charge. If we're fast, we can do this, and plug it in the room and charge it.'

Nooooooo. You can't be having this conversation. I'm not dead. I know what you're up to. And I hope as hell it doesn't run out of charge, whatever it is, or I will hunt you down.

In seconds, I'm being sped down the corridor and bumped into a lift. It's like those racing car video games, and the accompanying soundtrack is me going, 'Aaaaaaaa'. Because it's like my brain and my vocal chords are working. And nothing else.

The lift stops at my floor. I hear a male voice, 'Aila, yeh kya mast floor hai?' (Dude, what is this fabulous floor?!) A female voice answers, 'First time hai idhar?' (Is this your first time here?). Male voice continues to exclaim and ooh and ahh. And now I'm laughing inside my head, while my mouth is still going aaaaaaah.

Also, going under was so smooth and coming out of general anaesthesia was nothing like that. It was like trying to clamber out of a large sloping pit filled with jelly. It wasn't nice at all. My face kept feeling like it was on fire, while my body was going around in circles in a heavy fog. I was cranky, and every time I tried to speak, I would want to puke. Thank god for Anirban, who was fanning my face, holding my hand, patting my forehead. I would look at him through my haze, sitting there beside me, his eyes shutting in exhaustion, patting my face, and I would want to hug him to bits. But all I could do was moan in my irritation of wanting to come out of this, and the pain. But then a nurse came in with a cool trick. They had a machine set up next to me, and when the pain was unbearable, all I had to do was press the button on a remote she put in my hand, and slowly the pain would subside. I have no idea what the painkiller was, but I'd like to think it was morphine.

Also, in case you're thinking I gassed myself silly, apparently you can keep clicking, but the machine only delivers so many metered doses.

The next few days in hospital were full of learnings. To start with, they put a catheter in me during the surgery. I was dreading it. Peeing into a pipe and a bag. But it wasn't so bad. You never have to get up in the middle of the night to pee. Hurrah! Flip side, you can't do potty. It feels too weird. Try it. Hold your pee and try doing potty, it's impossible.

Then comes 6 a.m., the magic hour in hospitals. I don't know what is with their fascination for doing everything at that unearthly hour. So, my IV was put in at 6 a.m. My catheter was taken out at 6 a.m. My first medicine was given at 6 a.m. Oh my god. Just stop. Let the patient sleep. All that's needed is a roll call parade, so you feel like you're in jail!

The port. Ugh. I woke up the next day after surgery and looked at myself in the phone camera. There was a small dressing near the base of my throat. I peered at it, and almost dropped my phone. I could see the outline of a pipe under my skin. It went right down and connected to a small ball-like shape just over my right breast. This was the port.

And that's why the doctor asked me if I wore plunging necklines! Because this ball would jut out of my body for almost two years. Yes, my port stayed even after my chemo and radiation got over. As an extra caution, in case I needed it again. Just so you know, a chill goes down my spine every time I even write this.

Not that the port was painful, in fact it gave me a lot of entertainment. When people would stare at my chest, I could never tell if it was my boobs they were looking at, or that little golf ball that looked like it would start throbbing any minute.

Right now, I looked far from anyone who would ever wear a plunging neckline. I looked like a cyborg, plus my short hair was standing up. I shut the phone camera real quick.

And then there's the reconstruction. I have bandages all over me. And I kept feeling like my bra is very tight on one side. Then I'd realize I'm not wearing one. It's surgery feels! The tissue is trying to sort itself out, the nerves are all trying to join or connect, and I keep feeling tingling sensations. My armpit has been opened up to remove lymph nodes, so I can't feel too much of my upper arm. There's no pain after the first night, just some new sensations. I am also the original bag lady; one bag is attached to the pipes on my left side that drains the excess tissue, the other pipe is a pee bag. I'm paranoid the pee bag will fill up and splosh all over the floor, so I ask all visitors when they come in to bend and check how much pee there is in the bag.

No wonder I don't get too many repeat visitors.

And because they grafted some skin from my back to cover the nipple area, it feels like my back is stapled up. More tightness and more feeling like a python just wrapped itself around me and is slowly squeezing me to death.

Which brings me to this question. How do people get boob jobs? Or nose jobs? Or lip jobs? Or any jobs? How do they voluntarily sign up for all the discomfort and pain? Hats off to them.

Pamela Anderson, you have my respect.

So now I have a brand-new boob, but I also have so much dressing on my chest that if I lie straight, I could pass off as an Egyptian mummy. No bra is going to fit me, least of all my fancy ones with underwire. Which I am not allowed to wear for a while anyway. Ziba comes back with some plain bras and an incredible thing which is a small piece of cloth, fitted with hooks. Basically, it's a bra expander. Add this to the hooks of your bra and it gives you about two inches more of space around your back. Who thought of this? I would like to meet him or her, and thank them.

And finally, doctors can cure anything. Including stress and worry. My parents, who of course visit me every day at the hospital, are looking more and more miserable by the day. All those tubes, dressing, stitches, IV injections, it's taking a toll on them. And they feel helpless. It's like Anirban has a purpose, which is looking after me. But Mom and Dad are feeling like they are drifting. Till one afternoon, Mom gets up and says, 'We are going to meet your doctor.' They march off. And half an hour later, they return with big grins on their faces. Seriously, I think it's the first time I saw them smile in five days. Mandy has not just spoken to them and explained everything, but also told them great things about me. And that, ladies and gentlemen, is a trick that always works with parents. A good report card!

Surprisingly, the hospital stay wasn't so bad. Maybe because I was so determined to get out of there fast, and I was still in the zone. I think I was willing my body to hurry up and heal. Mandy would come in to see me every day, and look mighty pleased to see me on my laptop, or walking around in the corridor. Dr Quazi and his cyclonic gusts of cologne were holding me back. It's because of the reconstruction that I had to stay two extra days.

What also helped was my obsession with item songs at that moment. Oinx bought me a small speaker, and I would blast a Badshah playlist all day. In the evenings my chief cheerleaders would come and play Uno with me, and we'd do the Lungi Dance. No, I am not proud of it, but hey whatever gets you through a surgery.

It was Sunday afternoon when they let me go. I came back home in my favourite blue pants, blue shirt, and lilac converse sneakers. And, of course, a plastic packet holding my two drain bags. The pipes were still attached. Dad had put a 'Welcome Home' sign on the door.

I was in great spirits, because this felt like a breeze. The surgery happened, the surgeons did their job, the bad cells were out of me.

What I didn't realize was coming home would be hard. I was out of the zone that had seen me through.

First came the fact that it was difficult to adjust to being home. I'd keep thinking my drainpipes had moved and the bag wasn't filling. By the first evening, I was flipping out. I was sure something had gone wrong. The plastic surgeon didn't give me his number, my onco surgeon did. Mandy told me that even if no one takes your call, he will. I wanted to call him, but I didn't want to be that wuss who calls the surgeon every time she freaks out. So, I stayed put.

The night was difficult. You can only sleep on one side, because the other side has tubes that are going into you. Then you have to make sure your tubes and drains are hanging in a particular way so that it can all collect in the bag, and you don't thrash around while sleeping. Add my paranoia to that, and it was a bad night.

Morning was worse, because the drain bags had to be emptied, and Anirban had to check and note the amount that had drained out. For some reason, watching the nurses do it was okay. But watching

Anirban do it, I would feel light-headed. Then came having a bath. Anirban would have to sponge me in such a way that I didn't get one side wet. But before that he'd have to change my dressing. And every morning, that was my cue for a meltdown.

When I look back, I realize the one person who saw me through everything was of course Anirban. But it wasn't just seeing me through, it was like we both lived it. In the hospital, I'd be all happy and chirpy all day, and then before I slept something would trigger a meltdown. Some days I would be feeling scared, some days I would be wanting to just go home. And every night, Anirban would hold me and we'd both cry.

The morning dressing change when I got home was exactly like that. I just could not look at what they had done to me. The reconstructed breast was full of stitches that looked like dog bites. My back was just one big glaring scar and stitches. And the thing that set me off was when Anirban would carefully remove the gauze under the dressing, there would be blood. My breast had been scrapped so fine from inside that in places the skin was barely there. It felt like the slightest touch and it would tear. Then there was the nipple area, all that remained there was a patch of skin, stitched in a circle. The skin looked mottled and dark, like it had gone bad. I couldn't look at it. I felt like someone from a horror movie. Just scars and blood and stitches. This was not me. It would take me an hour to just mentally prep myself every day to take a bath, and get my dressing changed.

Then there was Mom and Dad. It was a tough time for them. Mom threw herself into cleaning and Dad barely spoke. He just looked sad all the time. I think they were already worrying about the chemotherapy. And imagine if I couldn't bear to see all the stitches and the blood, what it would do to them. As I write this, my heart is filled with love and gratitude for Anirban. I don't know how he did everything. Take care of me, manage my parents, go to work. It's just incredible. I owe him my life.

I realized then, as much as I love my parents, and I want to protect them, I have to first protect myself. Getting better fast was the best thing I could do for them. If I could not handle their grief, then I would need to tell them that. Even now it seems so harsh, and I have tears as I write this, but then, it was the best thing to do. I had to banish every negative thought and emotion.

The sword hanging over my head was obviously chemotherapy. I was supposed to see Mandy as soon as the lab reports from my surgery came in. In the meantime, I went to the hospital every second day to get the excess fluid drained from my back. It was weird, because the doctor would tap my back and ask if I felt anything. And I'd be like, no, nothing at all. The doctor would then put a needle into my back and do the draining. Imagine, having a needle go through and not feel a thing. That's how my back was, all nerves torn and numb. Everything, including my reconstructed breast, was just a tight ball of flesh with no feeling at all.

And then came the day of my test result. So, when they operated on me, the cancerous lump and lymph were sent for another biopsy and tests, on the basis of which the doctor would know what caused the cancer and what would be the appropriate protocol. So, we head out to Kokilaben Hospital, which I have now started referring to as Koks. Why be all formal when almost everyone there has seen your boobs.

We pick up the lab reports and make our way to Mandy. First, I have something to tell him. All these days, when I would be asked that standard question, 'Has anyone in your family had breast, ovarian or uterine cancer?', I would blithely answer no. I had heard that my uncle had stomach cancer and so did my grandmom from my mother's side. But one day, after surgery when I'm home, I ask Mom what happened to my grandmother. And she says she had ovarian cancer. I am aghast. I had no idea. Why didn't we ever speak about it? Nupur, my breast cancer survivor friend, told me that gynaecological cancers

are related. Which means Mom and I were always at a higher risk.
But it just never struck us.

I tell this to Mandy, and he makes a note of it. I'm glad he doesn't
judge me, but it really makes me think about how little we talk about
cancer, and how much of a taboo it is. It only strengthens my resolve
to talk about it, on my social feed, to friends, strangers, anyone. A
friend who heard about my diagnosis called me, and told me how
her mother had breast cancer, and she never told anyone. Not even
her own sisters and brothers.

Anyway, back to Mandy. Who tells me that I am ER positive.
Which means the cancer cells grow by feeding off the oestrogen
hormone in my body. And the protocol for this is … ta-da …
chemotherapy. Sixteen rounds of it.

My eyes widen. Sixteen rounds of chemotherapy.

Four rounds with a twenty-one day gap between them. And
then twelve rounds of weekly chemo. Followed by twenty rounds of
radiation.

Mandy is writing out everything. Anirban asks Mandy, 'Does
she need to go through all of this?' Mandy firmly says, 'Yes, it's fairly
standard, this protocol.'

He also says he doesn't like having too much of a gap between
surgery and chemo. Usually, there's a two-week gap for the body to
recover and they can start on the chemo. So, I should be ready to start
my protocol next week. He reaches out for the phone, then stops and
tells me he's going to put me on to the medical oncologist who will
handle my treatment. And do I have a preference? I just say, 'I'll go
with whoever you suggest.'

He picks up the phone and enquiries which doctor is around that
day. And the answer is Dr Imran. Mandy puts the phone down and
says, 'Great, go meet Dr Imran. I think he'll be good for you.'

And that's it. The biggest agni pariksha of my life so far, and it's
only a week away. I don't know at this point which should be called
the Big C, the cancer or the chemo.

We both go and meet Dr Imran. He's a nice, smiling doctor. He tells me there's nothing to worry about. And they'll start it off at the end of the week, on Saturday. I should not pause my life, I should do everything I love, and not lock myself in a room. The only thing I need to be careful about is not getting an infection or a cold, because that will interrupt my chemo schedule.

My head instantly goes into a spin. If they ever had a cold championship, I'd be the winner. I get a cold from anything—too hot, too cold, too dusty, too dry, too happy, too sad. The answer to everything is a cold.

He also tells me that chemo is far easier now, and that people will tell me all sorts of things, and I should totally disregard it. I nod. I am already terrified. I ask him if I'll be pukey and sick all the time. He says it depends from person to person. Some people get none of that. And hopefully I'll be one of those people.

Great. He's telling the truth. And that's not really comforting!

I ask him if I'll lose my hair. And he says yes, I should be prepared for that.

Armed with the plain facts that don't at all look appealing, we walk out. Anirban and I sit in Starbucks, and we talk. The most important thing is, how do we prepare ourselves? Anirban's parents are getting impatient with this forced holiday and want to come back home. My parents are having a tough time dealing with my impending chemo.

I think about what I want. I want to enter this peacefully. Without worry or stress. If the doctor has said some people don't get affected, I want to believe I am one of those people. I want to help my body. In fact, now I am determined to do this.

I tell Anirban I'm going to tell Mom and Dad the chemo will start later, and they should go back to Delhi for now. Let his parents come back. They will not know what's wrong with me.

Just then Koeli didi calls. I tell her that the chemo is in a week. And she offers to come. She says we'll paint and draw, and peacefully embrace the chemo. I like the idea of that. She's an artist, and has the soul of a free spirit. I instantly feel like she'll be a great distraction for me.

So, it's settled.

The next few days are like living in limbo. I literally have a week to live my life to the fullest. Plus, it's also my birthday that week. Mom and Dad are not happy I am sending them off. Anirban has a lot of work, which he's trying to complete before my chemo comes along. He doesn't know how much time off he'll need then. So Oinx steps in, and decides that the two of us should go see a movie on my birthday.

I love the movies, and I especially love movie halls. And I don't know when I'll be able to go to one next, so I jump at the plan. There's a new movie in town called *October*, and we manage to get tickets for it. It's only when we start watching the movie that we realize it's about a girl who goes into a coma, and most of the movie is set in a hospital, and she never comes out of the coma! It was a great movie, but such bad timing. It's like when I was in the hospital, the night before my surgery, I downloaded a book on my Kindle. Thinking just a couple of pages, and I'll fall asleep. The first book by the author was a funny rom-com, so I'm thinking this new one will be the same, perfect for before surgery. Only this one is about a cancer patient. I quickly go to the last page. She dies! What the fuck. Why can't these books come with a warning? And why can't authors just stick to one genre?

I have also adopted Himanshu and Nupur as my cancer guides. Of course, both have totally different advice to give. Himanshu tells me that I should eat to my heart's content before chemo starts. Because it'll rob me of my appetite, apart from the cravings that I might have. He craved pizza and Coke. Nupur on the other hand tells me to start juicing, and eating healthy greens every day, especially carrots. I decide to listen to both of them. So, I'm literally stuffing my face with pizza one minute and having carrot juice the next.

Apart from Himanshu and Nupur, I have a lot of other people giving me advice. It reaches a point where I start asking people a few minutes into them giving me advice, 'Have you had cancer?'

Silence. Followed by a no.

'Then if it's okay with you, I'd rather follow my onco's advice.'

I have variations to this. 'Are you an oncologist?' 'Have you ever successfully treated a cancer patient?' 'Where did you do your MBBS?'

Disclaimer: I am not so cool, I only said a lot of this in my head, while rolling my eyes. And quickly found a way to firmly tell them that I am only and strictly following my onco's advice.

There was a friend, who took it upon herself to call me persistently, and tell me not to do chemotherapy. Why? It would kill all my good cells.

Great point. But what about my bad cells?

She had a solution. A fantastic doctor, who was curing her friend via juices and Ayurvedic medicines. Her friend had stage four cancer. I was aghast. I clearly told her that I love everything organic, and Ayurvedic, and new wave and old wave, but this is cancer. I am not going to be taking any chances, thank you. She calls me thrice in that week to try and convince me not to listen to my onco and opt out of the chemo.

Finally, I'm borderline rude when I tell her I have made up my mind, and she needs to stop calling me, because it's stressing me out.

She gets the message.

She calls me two months later, to say she's so glad I didn't take her advice. Her friend died.

I am beyond rolling my eyes now. And that's the thing I learn through the course of my treatment. My medical onco is right. Everyone reacts differently to everything, surgery, chemotherapy, radiation. There is no one template. So, everyone who has someone who's been through it, and dispenses advice based on that, should be totally ignored.

I instead focus on two things.

First one is answering the damn doorbell.

Seriously, it is a curse to be at home. The doorbell rings all the bloody time. It's like someone put out a word to every single courier, postman, dog walker, security guy, internet guy. Go ring that bell they said. And ideally ring it between 2.30 and 5 p.m. As a result of which I had given up on the thought of ever sleeping in the afternoon.

Of course, I could call an electrician and figure out how to get the doorbell disabled. Though, with my luck, he would only come between 2.30 and 5! You need the patience of a saint to be home.

And of course, saint brings me to the second thing I decided to focus on.

Which was being my own Sri Sri.

I had to get into the zone. And unlike the surgery, where I had decided that it was the doctors who were going to bring this ship home, this time it had to be me. So, I actively seek out a yoga teacher. She's someone I've never met before, but I just like how she is on Instagram. Yep, judge a book by the cover. I reach out to her, and she's perfect. She doesn't freak out that I'm a cancer patient. She doesn't just look at me and say we'll meditate. She sees my stitches, my dressing, understands that I cannot put weight on one hand, and yet she extracts a lot out of me. She also loves nature and has a way with plants, so we decide that my sessions will be held in a park near my house, under a couple of palm trees.

It's beautiful. I don't know yet if I'll be able to do yoga through chemotherapy, but to do it post-surgery is marvellous. You are looking at your body, you are watching it as it learns to stretch, and move again. And it's like you and your body fall in love.

I told you I was being my own spiritual guru. So bear with me.

I devised my own method of visualization. I would lie flat on my yoga mat. And I would visualize myself going through my body, all the bloodstreams, veins, organs, and then I would talk to my body. I would tell it that the chemo was here to help. And it was necessary to make friends with it. I would also ask my body to protect the good cells, so the chemo could only destroy the bad cells.

I know it all sounds flaky and even a little childish, but it helped me. I'd feel very happy and positive after doing this. Like my body and I were a team.

It's strange, my taste in music also changed. From hardcore Hindi item songs, I started listening to Indian classical music. It's like my body and my mind would tell me where to flow, and I'd just go with it.

Going with the flow also meant coming to terms with the fact that my hair would fall. I decided that I'd buzz my hair to the shortest I could. Having that chic short bob was not going to help when my hair starts falling off in tufts, or at least that's how I imagined it. My friends came over, one of them is a hairstylist. She brought her shaving tools, and we played Kumar Gandharva loudly as she took off my hair. I cried when it was over, and they let me. Without hugging me or saying it'll be okay. I was allowed to grieve and say goodbye to what I was.

23

ω

The first chemo.

I woke up early. We planned to leave for the hospital by 8 a.m. Shaoli, who had her thalassemia transfusions at the same chemo ward, had already briefed us. The earlier we went, the faster we could get everything started, and the sooner we'd be out of there.

I wanted enough time in the morning to do my visualization, and not rush through stuff. This was an important day, stress levels were through the roof, I wanted to get into turtle mode.

Now picture this: my house has an open kitchen that looks into the living room. So, there was breakfast being cooked, because who goes for anything life changing without fried eggs in their stomach? The dog was impatiently waiting to go for his walk. The cat was trying to trouble the dog. Anirban was getting everything ready for the hospital. And in the middle of all that, to the smell of fried eggs, was me lying on my yoga mat, telling my body and my good cells that it was time to shake hands with the chemo.

I was calm. No butterflies, no exam hall feeling. I had cracked this, because I had a plan. I was going to embrace the chemo by coming home and countering the side effects with meditation and superfood shots. Basically, I was going into this, wanting to replicate an Ayurvedic spa experience. Completely lunatic plan, but at that time it sounded totally doable.

Oinx was coming with Anirban and me, even though we had no idea if anyone would be allowed inside. I was hoping the chemo ward would be like the movies, giant La-Z-Boy chairs with a personal screen where I could play games while they hooked me up to the medicines.

Turns out, the chemo ward wasn't anything like that. It's a giant ward, crammed with beds, one after the other. Think of it like an aircraft. Aisle in the centre, and beds on both sides. Only thing is, each bed has a plastic curtain that you can pull around it, for privacy. So now delete aircraft from your head, and think shower stalls, one after the other. That's your chemo ward.

Anyway, we reach the hospital, finish the formalities (which is a good way of saying pay through our noses), and then holding many forms and a wrap-around wristband with my name and details on it, we spend about ten minutes trying to figure out where the ward is. Turns out it's on the seventh floor, with big windows and a view of a large, bustling road. Which feels pretty weird, because you're getting pumped with chemicals, thinking this will be my life for the next nine months, and outside it's business as usual.

Anyway, we get there, and the nurses realize I am a newbie. A majority of them are Malayali, which I find very reassuring. Maybe because I have the chance to use the only Mallu word I know, chechi, which means older sister. Bingo! I hit the jackpot by knowing the only word that I would need for the next couple of months. They patiently guide me through the formalities of weighing myself, then registering and getting more tags for my wrist. Then, since I'm super early, I get to choose my bed. Another pro tip, courtesy Shaoli, is to get a bed closest to the nurse's station. So you can get their attention, and get your chemo started as soon as possible.

As my chemo progresses, there's a lot of thought that goes into which bed I should take. The beds near the loo are a no-no. The beds in the corner are also a no, because I don't want to be staring at a blank wall. The beds with a patient on either side is a risk, because you don't know how chatty, grumpy, or inquisitive they could be.

So I go with Shaoli's recommendation, and usually end up on the bed that's right on the aisle. At the end of every bed is a chair for the caregiver. On that day, I have two caregivers. The nurses are lenient, even though there's a sign saying only one is allowed. Oinx and Anirban manage to find another chair. I chat with them, while the nurses stream in and out of my shower stall, taking my blood pressure, blood oxygen, etc. Finally, my medical onco, who will henceforth be known as chemo doctor, arrives. He's all chirpy. My blood results are okay, and he declares me fit to take chemo.

I figure that they are first going to pump me with steroids, and then with two chemo drugs, one after another. The steroids are to help combat the side effects. But just in case, he also writes a list of emergency medication for fever, diarrhoea, nausea etc., and hands it to Anirban. In my head, I scoff at this list. Chemo doctor has no clue that I have this under control. Wheatgrass shots and some calming chamomile are all I am going to need. Looking back, I marvel at my misguided confidence. Or maybe the cancer survivor lady who told me I was in denial was right. I knew that it wasn't cancer lite, but I was hoping it would be chemo lite.

Also, now is the time they are going to make use of the port. But first, I've made a rookie mistake. I wore a kurta. And they need to stick the needle and IV into my port and keep it there, without any obstruction. So reluctantly, I changed into the open-front hospital shirt, which is a bit depressing since I do not look good in a Chinese collar, plus it reminds me that I am a patient. In fact, let me tell you, I have been put-off Chinese collars and paisley prints for life.

Now comes the port. A cool party trick. The port nurse is like a Malayali Uma Thurman from *Kill Bill*, who comes in scrubs. Before she arrives, another sister comes in, pulls the shower curtains around my bed in one decisive action, and sets everything up. The cutlery box I saw in the operation theatre? They have the same steel box wrapped in a blue cloth out here.

The nurse unwraps it and inside, in a kidney shaped tray, lie these gleaming steel bowls. The part of my brain that controls my middle-class domestic goddess side starts to ping. What lovely, shiny katoris. Perfect for dahi.

The nurse splashes disinfectant into them, and my port area is wiped clean. Then my Mallu Uma Thurman enters. She stands there, beside my bed, hands outstretched. The other nurse puts the scrubs over her, ties it, and then pours sanitizer over her hands. It's like I can hear church organ music playing in the background. We're prepping for something momentous. Uma waits for a minute, then shakes her hands and picks up the needle. Connects it to the IV pipe, flicks it, and then in one precise and fast jab, sticks it straight into my port.

Lucky for me, Uma is a pro, I don't feel anything. The port itself is a medical marvel. First of all, the veins on my hands are very thin, which means getting the chemo medicine to go through them would have been agonizing as hell. In fact, I know people who have had plastic surgery on their hand after chemo. It leaves so many scars and causes swelling. Thanks to the port being connected to a large vein, you don't feel the chemo going through at all. You can sit or lie down or chat and sometimes you even forget there is a needle going into your chest.

Now that the port is in, my steroids and medication start and then, ta-da, it's time for chemo. They kick it off with a drug called the Red Devil that looks like a glass bottle filled with Rooh Afza. I don't feel anything. I'm taking pictures. Talking to Oinx and Anirban. I'm all good. Next comes another drug. And finally, the flush that cleans my port and completes the treatment. It takes around five hours, and I'm feeling fine. But I'm obviously wound up inside, I'm looking for every single sign that my body will give me.

I leave the chemo ward. That's one down, out of sixteen. I have six months more of this to get through.

Other than a little chalky taste in my mouth, I feel okay, and I'm still sticking to my 'tackle chemo like a hipster' plan. On the way home, I call a café near my house and ask them to have my fresh wheatgrass shot ready. We stop on the way, they give me the glass through the car window, and I down it in one go.

We get home, and Koeli didi and a friend of mine called Khursheed, who will take me through the guided mediation, are waiting for me. Everyone is watching me anxiously, I can tell. For one crazy moment, I actually think that I should just pretend to drop to the ground and freak them all out. But no, it's too morbid, even for me.

I change my clothes, wash my face, tell Khursheed to get ready to start the meditation. I lie on my mat, open my eyes, and realize everyone is still looking at me. They are so sweet, to go along with my madcap idea. I grin and tell them, 'I am fine.'

And that's when the nausea hits me.

Oh boy, it's bad. First of all, I hate nausea. I could deal with the surgery and the injections, but this pukey feeling is the worst. I sit up, drink some water, and try meditating again. But let me tell you, there is no way you can focus on your breathing when all you want to do is stick a finger down your throat and bring it all out.

I sit up again. Anirban has got a whole box of medicines that the chemo doctor wrote out as emergency supplies. This includes stuff for nausea. Didi is patting me, holding my head. Anirban is rushing about getting a bucket for me to puke into, Khursheed is standing against the wall, looking really freaked out and asking me, 'How are you feeling?'

How am I feeling? Like I'm going to hurl everything I've eaten. All that horrible hospital food I ate today, including the depressing black custard which seems to be their patented sweet dish. Like it's all stuck in my throat. Like I want to cry. Is this what chemo is going to be like? How will I get through six months of this?

Then it strikes me. This is not the chemo, this is the wheatgrass shot.

I tell Didi and Anirban that. My head is in the bucket, I am trying to puke and I'm telling them, 'Don't blame the chemo. It's a friend. It's the wheatgrass shot.'

They don't look too convinced, but don't say anything. I'm lucky Anirban loves me, and Didi is equally mad.

Finally, I have a little puke festival. It's all green and wheatgrass flavoured. I can smell it, and I've never been happier. Because hurrah, I was right. My plan didn't work, but at least it's not the chemo that's trying to kill me.

I take all the emergency medicines and pass out. Content in the knowledge that my body and the chemo are starting to be friends.

The next week is a little woozy. First, I smell of chemicals. Especially when I pee, I'm like those factories that are polluting our rivers. I have to close my nose, because that smell makes me nauseous. Also, I feel unsettled in the morning, foggy, sleepy, and very slow. Didi makes it a routine to come downstairs early. I fall asleep with my head in her lap, and she sings to me. She and Anirban, they are watchful and they give me space. So I can get time to understand how my body and mind are dealing with it. That's very important to me. Remember, control freak. But also, if I can't process it myself, and only go with the anxiety that everyone gives off when they hear the word chemotherapy, how will I find what is my experience?

Second, I start falling to pieces the morning after chemo, when I have to remove the dressing on my port. It's very minor, and I need to take it off before I have a bath. But I'm shaking and crying, because it brings back memories of the blood and the mottled skin under my dressing after my surgery. And more than that, it makes me look at my breast, the reconstructed one. Criss-crossed with stitches, raw skin and no sensation, it feels like this is not a part of my body. It's like I have two breasts. One I've known for forever. I know how it feels, how it becomes tender when my periods are coming, what it weights when I hold it. And the second one is this battered and bruised lump of flesh and tissue, that I don't recognize or know at all. I don't even want to touch that breast. Of course, when I mention this to my onco, he patiently explains to me that I must touch it, it is my breast, and my tissue. But I just can't.

Instead, I focus on what I can tackle. My body and the chemo. I am hell-bent on this Best Friends Forever thing. And slowly, by the second week the fog recedes, and I start feeling like myself. I set a routine for myself. I pretend this is like those war movies, where I'm a prisoner who has been thrown into solitary confinement and my only way to keep sane is sticking to a routine.

I drink smoothies, stuff beetroot and carrots by the kilo down my face, because somebody tells me they've got cancer fighting properties. I don't really care for steamed and mashed food. But right now, I'm keeping an open mind and trying everything. This includes listening to meditation chants, trying hemp oil, doing yoga. The more stuff I do, the better I feel. It's like life still hasn't gone out of me. My friends come every evening, and we play Uno and order pizza. I'm thinking that I can go back to work soon. My appetite is just fine. And it looks like I'm one of those people who chemo will not affect.

Here's the thing. The minute that thought crosses your mind, reality jumps at you.

Three weeks are up, and it's time for my second chemo. My hair is still holding out, and I look and feel like I did before my chemo started. So secretly, I am beginning to believe I've got this. My visualization and chemo-body BFF theory are working. And I dare say, I'm not like everyone else. Ghanta!

This time around Ziba is coming with Anirban and me. And I'm not making a rookie mistake of wearing a closed top. I'm wearing a shirt with buttons. It's back to the chemo ward, back to finding a good bed, and back to having my port hooked up to all the medicines. I am feeling relaxed. Anirban and Ziba are making me laugh by giving points to the chemo doctors on the basis of clothes, bedside manner etc.

The chemo gets over, and we are on our way home. I'm feeling woozy. This time the wooziness hits as soon as I leave the hospital. I'm also hungry. I haven't eaten much of the hospital food. Even though there was no black custard this time, I can't get it out of my head. So, I open my favourite food delivery app, and I order myself a quinoa burger. I obviously don't learn from past mistakes. I have totally banished wheatgrass from my life, but it never strikes me that I need to eat light on the day of chemo. I am so hell-bent on being hipster mata.

I reach home, wash up. This time I notice one more thing. The chemical smell has spread, it's not only in my pee, it's now on my body and even my clothes smell strange. By the time I register this, my burger arrives. I chomp it down, eat the hummus that goes with it, take my nausea tablet in two hours' time, and pass out.

When I wake up in the morning, my stomach feels strange. Anirban has just woken up, and he's in the kitchen, heating water for his coffee. I go to the loo, and I have an upset stomach. I know that one of the things the chemo doctor told me is that I might have an upset stomach or even diarrhoea. I'm not really worried, I just need to take my emergency medicines. I come out of the loo to tell Anirban this.

But by now I'm also feeling very pukey. And it feels like my stomach is not okay at all. So I get back to the loo. And that day turns into a nightmare. I go to the loo twenty-two times. That's not diarrhoea, that's Yamraj waving at me. I can't stand, I can't walk. I'm falling down on the pot. Anirban is giving me medicines, wiping my face, and even holding me while I'm on the pot. The smell of shit, chemicals, sweat is all over. I am crying, I can't cry any more, I am like an animal. I just lie huddled, and then it starts all over again. Anirban's coffee remains untouched.

The emergency medicines are clearly not working. Anirban messages the chemo doctor. Who sounds wary, and says this could be a side effect of chemo. This bad? Even if I breathe, I need to shit or puke. By late evening Anirban is super worried, he calls Mandy. Mandy tells him not to worry. Says the chemo does affect some people like this unfortunately. And we should wait and watch till tomorrow morning.

Damn. How the mighty have fallen. From the people it doesn't affect, I've gone straight to the people it does.

It's night. I'm drifting in and out of sleep. My mouth tastes terrible. I look over, Anirban has passed out in exhaustion. All the lights are on in the house. I shut my eyes, and my stomach is ready to give way again.

I don't have the heart to wake up Anirban. I slide off the bed, I crawl to the bathroom on all fours. I don't shut the door, I'm scared I might faint or pass out. I somehow manage to sit on the pot. When it's over, I sleep on the bathroom floor.

It's the worst night I have ever seen. At some point I make it back to the bed. And then it starts all over again. This time I manage to call out to Anirban.

By morning, he's got dark circles and is looking haggard. I've lost the will to live. I'm only moaning. If this is chemo, I don't want it. I can't go through it. Anirban calls Mandy early in the morning. I'm crying, and begging Anirban to take me to the hospital. Mandy tells him to start me on ORS and continue with the medicines.

Ziba has come, as reinforcement. Vijaya, the lady who has been working at my house for the past ten years, she's wiping my head. She lost a young son to cancer, so she's very protective about me. Ziba comes armed with a bottle of No 77 eau de cologne. I have no idea how Ziba is so perfect at being the right person in an emergency. Who else would have thought of that? The smell brings with it whiffs of my childhood, and for a few minutes I'm at peace. She's dipping hankies in it and placing it on my wrists and forehead. I have some respite. And we think I've turned a corner.

But no. I can't even keep the ORS in. It's now over twenty-four hours. I really feel like I don't want this anymore. I'm crying because I am so frightened about how I'll go through the rest of the chemo. Ziba and Anirban are taking turns washing my face, pressing my hands and feet. I can tell they are also really scared now. Anirban is on the second day of half carrying me to the loo every twenty minutes. He calls Mandy again. Mandy asks him what I ate. And then prescribes antibiotics, saying it might be a stomach infection coupled with the chemo.

It takes another twenty-four hours of Anirban and Ziba taking turns to sit with me, pushing apple flavoured ORS inside me, holding me in the loo. After that, I slowly start to turn the corner. My stomach can hold liquids and then yoghurt and then toast. It was an infection.

Once I'm better, I still refuse to blame the chemo. And I strike quinoa burgers and hummus off my list as well.

But what also happens is, that second chemo changes everything for me. First, I quickly abandon my hipster notions and promptly turn to comfort food. My Bengali roots start showing as all I want to eat now is homemade rice, dal, and fish curry. I don't want to see another salad or ingredient that doesn't have a Hindi name!

My mom-in-law is thrilled. Every day, she'll make a simple fish curry or a light mixed vegetable with pumpkin and broad beans and spinach, and have it sent out to me. My appetite is raging. It's like the infection has emptied out my stomach and pushed my Bong genes to my taste buds. I want rice and fish, and more rice and fish!

Then, I want my parents. I want my mother to hold my hand and press it, and I want my father to keep stroking my head. Both Anirban and I realize that we need Mom and Dad to see me through my chemo. Even if it is hard for them to see me like this, they still want to. And I begin to realize that I can't protect them from this. They are parents, they want to be there. And I have to get over this desire to be the best daughter and spare them from pain. I have to let go of my misplaced guilt.

That's not all. That chemo also changes my mental make-up. I am scared of infections, of falling sick, of nazar. I can no longer eat outside food, I have to peel every fruit I eat. I don't want anyone to enter my bedroom with shoes or outside clothes. My dog, who I love to bits, I am now scared to hug him. I wear a mask everywhere I go, or when people come to visit me. I've seen what a simple infection can do, and I start freaking out at the slightest imbalance. I am no longer that happy-go-lucky woman who went into it thinking she's too cool for school, and she'll ace it. I'm now very aware of how precarious things can be.

24

Even now I can smell the apple ORS.

Till then, it was like we had a party. I think we had a party through your surgery, through your first chemo. But that second chemo, that's when I felt like I'm looking at cancer in the face, when I saw you that day in your home. I still get goosebumps talking about it. I just felt like now I'm seeing it, I didn't see it all these days.

It was very bad, I think because you were very ill. The loose motions you had that day, it was quite scary, and that's when I said, no man, this is not the big party we're making it out to be.

And slowly, by then, you had also started changing physically. Your hair was buzzed, you had started putting on that steroidal weight, and I could see ... I could see the toll the chemo was starting to take on your body.

Till then, it was so easy. You recovered so well from the surgery. You must have been going through more than any of us could see, but I felt it was okay till then. It didn't seem like cancer-cancer, till that day.

Till you were that ill, it almost felt like we could handle it. Then suddenly, it felt like it was beyond what we could handle.

Everything changed from that day. We knew you were fighting cancer.

—Ziba

181

25

ω

Considering I spent six months of my life dealing with chemo, I think I should talk about what it was like in detail. Our relationship status could be classified as 'trying desperately to be friends', where I was the desperate one, who was doing all the chasing. The chemo didn't give a shit.

To me there were two parts to chemo. One was chemo day care, which is what you start casually calling the chemo ward after a few turns. Everyone thinks it's a gloomy depressing place straight out of the dark ages, with huddled bodies crying softly in their beds.

Nothing could be further from the truth. In fact, my solution to normalize cancer and to remove the fear of chemo from people's minds is starting chemo day care visits for the aam janta. Many of my friends, who took turns to come with me for my chemo, were bowled over by how normal, and in fact even cheerful, the place is, under the circumstances.

Of course, you have to excuse the Indian habit of bringing a whole baraat with you when you come for chemo. The nurses would literally have to yell at people. Some days, the aisle between the beds would be so crowded with relatives, caregivers, and once even a pandit, that the nurses were like a dodgeball team that had been handed medicines and syringes. This is when there's a clear sign saying not more than one person per patient. But on the flip side, maybe that's also what makes chemo day care look less scary. It's the opposite of sterile, it's a compartment in the Indian railways.

What adds to that train journey feeling is the fact that most people, patients, and caregivers have never heard of something called earphones. They will chat with their broker, instruct whoever is doing the cooking at home, and listen to devotional music on speakerphone.

And pretty much in the same vein, there's no way people will not start chatting with each other in minutes. It doesn't matter if you are reading, not making eye contact, or have needles coming out of you, everyone will ask what happened, how long, who is your doctor, what you do, how many people are in your family. And finally, 'Bada dhakka laga hoga na?' ('Must have been such a shock, right?').

Nobody really expects the patient to answer. They'll look right past you and direct the questions at the caregiver. It used to irritate me earlier. Like, look at me. I am not dead, you idiot. But then I realized, they don't really want answers. It's just everyone bound together by anxiety. Like the outside of an exam hall, where you're waiting for your kid to come out.

I wouldn't be surprised to hear people have cracked business deals and marriage proposals in chemo day care.

As your chemo progresses, chemo day care just becomes part of your life. Like for six months, this is your office.

I used to come in, say hi to all the nurses, weigh myself, give them the details, and collect my band. Then grab my bed, all the while looking out for my chemo friends. Yes, I had chemo friends. Two women, also being treated for breast cancer. Our chemo days would sometimes coincide, so we'd look for beds next to each other. We'd chat and laugh, and discuss wigs and getting the plastic surgeon to fix our lips as an add on. We had nicknames for the doctors, and I would look out for this very cool doctor, who dressed brilliantly, wore heels, carried an iPad, and moved around in style. It was so good to see her. There were days that I could pretend I was in a meeting room and not a chemo ward when I saw her.

By now, I was also friends with the guy who looked after the bedding and sheets, and I always got an extra pillow. Anirban had also managed to get me a food pass from Mandy. Every chemo morning, he'd wake up early, and make me these yummy egg and tomato sandwiches with the softest bread and we'd carry that along with some fruits. He'd carry his laptop, and work at the foot of my bed. We settled into a routine.

I carried my Kindle to every chemo, but more often than not I didn't need it. Thanks to all the free entertainment. Like the lady who came with her brother and wife. They were obviously massive foodies, because they spent the entire time discussing food in elaborate detail. Couple of chemos down, I realized I had to find a bed that was far from her, because while I was okay with rajma and chole recipes being read out, I drew the line on hearing about boti kebabs while they were shoving the needle into my port. Plus, it made me very hungry.

There was also a gentleman who worked in films. Twice, I had the bed next to him. He'd be talking non-stop to his friends till his chemo doctor arrived. Then he'd go totally silent.

The doctor would ask him, 'Are you still smoking?'

Silence.

'I'm asking you if you are still smoking.'

Silence.

'Answer me!!!'

Silence.

At this point the doctor would lecture him loudly and tell him, 'What's the point of chemo or medicines, if you can't stop smoking?'

Once, the man tried to defend himself by saying he was eating thirty oranges a day, so that he got enough vitamin C to beat the cancer. The doctor pretty much lost his shit.

I used to love watching the different chemo doctors do their rounds. Each one had their own style of dealing with patients and showing tough love or sympathy when they had to. Some patients were clingy, some caregivers had enough questions to fill a GMAT paper, some were genuinely lost, and they dealt with everyone differently.

I remember there was a girl, who came with her parents and husband. It must have been her second chemo. The doctor stopped to ask her how she's doing, and the floodgates opened. She was pissed off as hell. And she started to complain. 'They are not letting me eat what I like. Not even normal food. They eat their food on the table, and I have to eat only boiled food in bed. They don't let me leave the room. They are saying I should rest. How can a person rest all the time? I will go mad. I told them I will tell you everything.'

The doctor turned to the family and gave them such a stern look that I almost pulled my shower curtain and hid. They got a massive dressing-down that day as the doctor steadily told them how superstition and treating the patient like she's got some infectious disease were bigger problems than the chemo. When I peeked at the girl, she looked so happy. It was like a scene from *Chak De! India*, all the patients within hearing distance were rooting for the girl and the doctor.

There was also a time when the head nurse requested me to go talk to a girl on her first chemo. The ward was relatively empty, and she was alone. By now I was on my tenth chemo, and I felt like an old hand. In fact, I was like those college dadas. If you've ever studied in Kolkata, you'll know what I'm talking about. These are guys who look like they could have two kids, but they are still in college. They never leave. They might be slow but they're really nice. Most will show you the ropes and be like an unofficial mentor for every batch. I felt like those dadas. All I needed was a cigarette and cup of tea as I walked into chemo day care and greeted the nurses by name, and waved to the ward boy and chatted with some old patients.

Anyway, before they could start my chemo, I went to chat with the girl. She was pretty sorted, and told me that she was going to get through this. I was impressed. And then she pulled out some pamphlets and tried to convince me to join her faith. I fled.

There were also the things that broke your heart. And that was always the kids at the chemo ward. With their worried parents. Most of them would take the beds at the end of the ward, and I'd pass them on my way to the loo. I could never meet their eyes.

And then there were things that exasperated me. Like they have two loos in the chemo ward, for about forty beds. That's about forty patients who need to keep going to the loo every thirty minutes, because the steroids and medicines make you want to pee a lot. Plus, maybe it's also the stress. Anyway, the math sucks in this case.

Here's how it went. Every time you wanted to pee, your caregiver or nurse would have to pick up your medicine bottle and hold it at a height, and walk with you and your IV to the loo, down the aisle crowded with caregivers. You looked like you were part of some strange wedding procession. Then you'd wear slippers with 'chemo day care' written on them. I hated it. I was convinced some people had splashed their pee on the slippers.

Once you gingerly stepped into the loo, the medicine bottle could be slipped over a hook at a height, near the pot, and you could do your business.

Problem was that how on earth was I going to sit on a pot that so many other patients had sat on, or even peed on! I am not joking. The seat cover isn't just yellow because it's old. The last thing I wanted was a urinary tract infection. So, I would have to resort to the helicopter.

Most women in our country know that one. Pee with your bum suspended over the pot, without touching it. Great for your thigh muscles but totally not great for a long, relaxed pee. Plus, your pee, thanks to the chemo medicine, smells like you set up a little chemical factory in your crotch. So, you are holding your breath, hovering mid-air over the pot, staring at slippers which you hope are wet with water and not pee, and you have an IV line attached to your chest. Whew! Not fun.

And that thing with holding your medicine bottle high? Because if you didn't, it caused something called 'back flow'. Where the blood from your veins started coming into your IV. The first time it happened to me, I almost fainted in fright. Till I realized the nurses were all chill, and this was just another chemo ward party trick!

The second part to chemo is how it felt and what it did to me.

The first day of chemo was always the worst. I'd be all fine till I finished my session and left the hospital. That's when the fog would start to roll in. That chemical smell would invade my nostrils, nausea would creep in … and it just felt like I was in space, walking and drifting in a vast ocean of black. By the time I got home, I'd start to feel like I was moving in slow motion. I'd lie down, and wait for it to pass. There was nothing anyone could do. All I could see in my head was that red medicine, the one I had laughingly called Rooh Afza. It haunted me. I would lie on the bed, sometimes in the dark, sometimes with the TV on, not really registering anything. Just waiting for 7 p.m., when I could pop my nausea medicine and pass out.

This physical aftershock happened during my big four chemos, the ones that had the twenty-one-day gap. Himanshu had told me something, which was playing out exactly as he described it. 'The first week will feel like shit, the second week you'll slowly start to recover, and by the third week you'll feel all chirpy and like yourself. Only, it'll be time to go back for the next round of chemo.'

The first week was always bad. It felt like I was living in a fog. There's no physical side effect. But you are mildly nauseous, your stomach feels funny, and it's like a horrible hangover that just refuses to go. I mean if I have to have a hangover, I'd like to be able to have the fun that comes before it. This is just cheating.

Plus, some smells just drove my nostrils crazy. Coffee, cologne, eggs frying. Ooh, I'd want to start retching immediately. At times I'd actually wonder if this was pregnancy or cancer.

Then came the stomach. I would never know what gift the next day will bring. Will it be loose motions, or will it be constipation? It's like the chemo was making a beeline for my gut. When I think about it, chemo robs you of certain things. Like your dignity. If it wasn't bad enough that Anirban and Ziba had to see me smelling of potty and sweat, and groaning and moaning, there was this other thing. Somewhere between my second and third chemo, I found I was constipated. The chemo doctor had told me this was another of the expected side effects. Eye-roll. It's like someone was opening a Pandora's box of side effects.

I'd never had constipation. Heck, I'd never had half the things that were happening to me. And I wasn't even prepared for them, because I had hardly done any reading or research. Going with the flow was literally biting my bum. And before I knew it, the constipation was so bad that it was hard to do potty. I wasn't used to it, and I was too embarrassed to tell anyone, so I'd strain and huff and puff till I started getting this terrible pain every time I sat on the pot.

After a couple of days of crying on the pot, I finally realized I couldn't handle this myself. I had to tell Anirban. As usual, he was kind and considerate, and didn't call me a prize idiot but made me call the chemo doctor.

Who had obviously seen a lot of this. And rather calmly told me, 'Could be a side effect. You may have developed an anal fissure, continue to have stool softeners and go see a general surgeon.'

What?!!! Now I have a fissure! And I have to find a general surgeon as well?

And he's going to look up my bum?

Where will I find this person? This called for a fresh round of tears.

There was only one thing to do. Call Mandy.

And this is why I think that Mandy is the best doctor in the world, because you are not just a cancer patient to him, you are a real person with anxieties, who is struggling. And he's the head of the breast cancer department, yet he takes my call and tells me what to do. He doesn't just brush me off and tell me to find a bum or fissure doctor. I have to apply a cream, in my ass. Shudder shudder. And sit in a tub with warm water mixed with potassium permanganate.

It's a hellish two weeks. I literally don't want to eat, so I don't have to do potty. I am terrified of sitting on the pot. But somehow, I suck it up. My parents and Anirban are watchful, but don't say anything. I guess they know I'm feeling miserable. And it's not just because I have a fissure and I have to tell them. It's because I am struggling. I can't understand how two months back, I was this person who looked so good, who felt so good, and now suddenly I have a breast that feels like a hard lump. I am nauseous all the time, I'm slow, and my bum is on fire.

Twice a day, I shut my bedroom door, put cling film on my finger, smear it with ointment, and shove it up my bum. I sit in the potassium water thrice a day. I make rookie lady-with-fissure mistakes, like reading the instructions on the ointment tube, which says the cap should be smeared with ointment and put up your bum. Guess what, never put a cap into your bum! It cut me, and made me bleed. More suffering, more crying, more loss of dignity.

Then of course, there's the hair. Oh my god, I could write a whole book on it. After my second chemo, I begged my parents to come. Both Anirban and I needed them, and of course parents being parents, without a word or without once saying 'told you so', they arrived. My hair was a spiky buzz cut, and it looked pretty chic. As usual, the super optimistic part of my brain had convinced the rest of me that this zero-cut will stay. It's too short to fall off. And I'll just look like Demi Moore in *G.I. Jane*.

I remember lying on the sofa, with my head on Dad's lap. He was absent-mindedly running his hand on my head. And my scalp started hurting. I wondered why. When I slept that afternoon, my scalp felt sore on the pillow. And that's because my hair had decided to give my optimistic side a tight slap.

That afternoon, when I got up, my pillow was covered with hair. Short, spiky hair. And in the next two days, it was all over my towel, my sheets, my clothes. It just kept falling, and before I knew it, there was nothing. Just my bald head.

In spite of thinking I'll be cool with it, I wasn't. Even now I wonder why it affected me so much. Maybe it's because everything was changing, my body, my face ... I felt unrecognizable. Like I didn't know who I was any more.

The first few days of being bald were especially tough. I remember my friends who I work with came to see me. This was the first time they'd see me looking like this, like a cancer patient. And I wore a cap, because I was so shy about the way I looked. I felt odd wearing it, like here I am in my living room, in the middle of the day, sweating in the Mumbai humidity, dressed like a rapper. I was awkward, and I just wanted them to leave. I didn't want them to see me like this, or see any sort of surprise or sadness in their eyes.

The bald head was also a sign for people to stare at me and give me pitying looks. I hated it. Then there were the 'we must cheer for cancer patients' people. Like the girl who would see me when I walked in the park near my house, and raise her hands and clap for me. I'd run even faster. I am not a freak show. I don't want you to clap and have others turn and look at me.

All I wanted was for people to not notice me, or not stare or sympathize. Just be normal, goddammit.

One time, I went to buy something from a shop near my house. An organic shop, where you'd expect people to have a little more exposure and, thereby, sensitivity. I always wore a mask when I went out, because I didn't want to catch an infection and screw up my chemo. I had calculated that my chemo and radiation cycle would be over by early December, which means I'd actually have reason to celebrate the new year. And I wasn't going to let anything derail that.

So, I'm buying things at this fancy store, with my bald head and my mask, and a lady just keeps staring at me. I'm at the vegetable section, she's looking at me. I'm buying butter, she's still staring. I'm choosing fruit, I can feel her eyes on me. Not even subtle, just straight staring. So finally, I walk up to her, lower my mask, and in a loud whisper, announce, 'I have cancer.' She left the shop faster than you can say bhindi.

There are things that shouldn't have been a big deal, but they were. A friend of mine used to call me Ganju affectionately, and I hated it. My parents were watching this show on Netflix, where the protagonist is a bald Israeli man called Doron, and they'd lovingly stroke my head and call me Doron. I hated that as well.

In fact, I had started to hate how I looked. There were days when I just wouldn't want to go near a mirror.

I often thought about wearing a wig, but this was Mumbai. I'd probably melt faster than all the ice caps in Antarctica. And also, everyone I know and I'm close to would know I'm wearing a wig. And that was just weird, like why would I be shy to show them what I really looked like?

On the one hand, I'd want to hide my head, and on the other, I'd go everywhere with my bald head. It was like I was constantly on a see-saw, testing myself. When my weekly chemo started, I decided to drop into the office. All these days, when the whole office would come together and video call me, I'd never show my face. Now I had this insane need to show it, to look at their reactions. I wore a sari and a bindi and nothing to cover my scraggy bald head. And even when I was going up in the elevator, to office, I kept thinking I should just turn and run. I don't want people to see me like this. I don't want to see the shock on their faces, even if it was fleeting.

It's not like people who know you or care about you want to look shocked, but it happens. Even they can't help it. Like the time I went to my kathak class in the middle of my chemo to say hello to my teacher. My teacher was incredible, there was no change in her reaction. But the other students, who had last seen me, with my long hair and massive grin and full-of-energy vibe, I saw that look in their eyes. That mixture of pity and awkwardness.

Now, when I look back, I think I should have just worn a wig, and saved myself a lot of heartache.

It would probably also have made the lady who lived in the flat above me happy.

One day, I'm waiting for the elevator, when she walks up to me, and asks how I'm doing and how sad she is that this happened to me. I immediately adopt my Saint Shormistha face, and with a half-smile, nod and tell her not to worry, because I'll be all good very soon.

She gives me some prasad. And then as we're riding up the elevator, tells me, 'Beta, tum scarf kyun nahi pehnte? Aajkal bade designs milten hain. Pehen liya karo.' ('Why don't you wear a scarf? Nowadays you get such nice designs, you should try it out.')

I loudly count to ten as I get off.

The problem with losing hair is not that you're left with a shiny smooth bald head. Not always, most times it's patchy, because it grows between chemos, and then falls again. I look like a baby hedgehog with a swollen face.

I'm changing. The carefree attitude I started off with is tempered. My body is feeling the strain. I'm putting on weight thanks to the steroids and my face is ballooning. And I'm struggling to accept all this.

Also, I had no idea that I'll lose my eyelashes and my eyebrows. It's such a small thing, look at the bigger picture, you're fighting the good fight, I tell myself every day. But as eyebrows go, and the lashes fall, I start looking more and more like a cancer patient. The dark circles, the pallor, no hair, no eyebrows or eyelashes, moon face, the hump in my neck. You can tell. And I just hate that. I do not want people to notice and then whisper to each other. Or quickly look away.

I want them to acknowledge it. Like my friend, Anand, who comes to see me. He walks into the house and straight up says, 'Okay, I want to know. What is it like? What are they doing to you? How long? Give the details.' It's a blessing. The truth is, everyone wants to know, but are so scared to ask. So, they just say something banal like 'How are you feeling?'

Ughhh. It's the worst question ever.

A friend of mine, Avanti, came to see me after my surgery. And when she was leaving, she hugged me and then pulled back and said, 'Shormu, how does the reconstructed breast feel?' I started laughing and asked her, 'Want to feel it?' And with full enthusiasm she did. We laughed, I called her a pervert, and it was great that with a childlike innocence, she asked me something she was curious about.

Wait, that brings me to something I need to talk about. A slight diversion. So, a lot of people have asked me what the reconstructed breast feels like. Time to get it off my chest. It feels good because it fills a bra, because it gives me cleavage, because when people see me, they have no idea that technically I don't have one breast. Or at least

I don't have the OG breast. But, I don't have any feeling there. It's like a dummy padded breast that's attached to my body.

Chemo also brings with it the gift of superstition. It's like someone turned on this switch in my head. Now if I say, 'Ooh, that looks yummy', immediately my head says, 'Don't say that.' Don't tempt the universe into thinking you love too many things, too much.

It's true. I love too many things. Almost all food is yummy. All plans are brilliant. Every book is something I have to read. And I'm not putting on an act. That is me.

But for the first time in my life, I start to curb my enthusiasm. It's sad. It's not me. To have this mental voice constantly and creepily telling me, 'Don't say you love things too much', is tiring.

I can't even say simple things without wanting to take them back. Like on a good day, I'm sitting on my mat and telling my yoga teacher how yoga is my saviour. And the minute it comes out of my mouth, the voice says, 'Stop, don't say that. Don't ever say it aloud that something means so much to you.'

I try to reason this out. Why is this happening? Do I think I tempted fate by being this person that loved everything too much? Is that why I think I got cancer? Am I scared that 'nazar lag gaya' (aka the good old evil eye) caused it? Or is it that I feel I loved so many things so much, that in the court of God they decided, 'That's it, let's control this one a bit. She's having too good a time.'

I figure it's the third one I'm worried about. I'm scared they'll take away the things I love.

So, I turn to a Bengali term that I used to hate. It goes like this.

Person: Kamon (How goes it?)

Typical Bengali reply: Bas, cholche (What to say … coming along).

Mind you, the reply is not 'bhalo' (good) or even a 'thik-thik' (okay-okay), but a non-committal, tempered with caution, 'bas, cholche'. Which basically translates to: life is dragging me along and I'm making do.

During my chemo, I had new respect for 'bas, cholche'. It's a great way to keep the evil eye away. When you tell the universe that everything is blah, the universe quickly goes, 'Na baba, not interested', and leaves you alone.

Cancer plays devious mind games. And for the first time in my life, my response to 'how are you' was a sigh, a pause, and then, 'Bas … you know how it is … coming along.'

Chemo has so many side effects. But the ones people don't talk about are these ones. Like superstition. Like losing your dignity and your independence.

And feeling jealous of your friends.

Aah, I'm so not proud of this at all. But I will also not judge myself, because dammit, I was going through a lot. But I was so jealous of small things. Like, for instance, a lot of my female friends would come to see me after work. And they'd come in their nice office clothes, with eyeliner and lipstick and looking all fly. And I'd hate it. I'd make excuses not to see them. It was a reminder of what my life used to be and how much it had changed. It's not their fault, even back then I knew that. It's not like they could put on weight and shave their hair and come looking grubby. But it was hard to see them.

And then there was Ziba and Oinx. Because of constantly coming to see me, and exchanging news on me, and basically surrounding me, they became friends. And sometimes, they'd stop for a beer after they met or they'd catch up somewhere, and I would hate it. Again, it's almost petty, but it's as if my mind was just turning me into something else.

A friend of mine sent me pictures of her vacation in the UK. And I was so snappy about it. My friends and colleagues would make plans to go drinking, eating, having farewell parties, and it was tough.

Tough to stand on the WhatsApp group sidelines and say, 'Have a great time, you people.'

Did most of my friends sense this? I'm guessing they did. But I think no one really understood why losing my hair was so traumatic to me. For a long time, even I didn't even understand why. But then I realized that it was a physical marker of the fact that I had cancer, and I had to see that marker every time I looked in the mirror, and that is something only I had to deal with. And understand.

I remember there was a time when a friend invited me for a party to her house, and some of my other friends were going. Of course, I said no. Because I couldn't eat outside food (you did read about the second chemo, right?), and because I didn't want to risk an infection or catch a cold. They were sweet and insisted that I could sit in another room, and even carry my own food. But I still refused. I felt like I'd be some sort of cancer item number, where everyone would be overly nice to me and feel sorry for me.

This balance between caring and sympathy is something I struggled with. Maybe I read too much into it. But when your pride and dignity take such a hit, you can't help being touchy, can you?

I was dealing with all this, when another bolt from the blue hit me. My periods stopped. Just after my second chemo, I kept waiting for my period to knock on my fallopian doors, and all I got was some stray spots of blood. Now, nobody tells you this stuff. Not your doctors, nurses, no one. Maybe they are pretty sure that people will google this.

I was doing nothing of that sort. I was busy organizing let's-get-to-know-you sessions between my body and the chemo. So anyway, I saw the spots and I freaked out. Where is my beloved period? I called the chemo doctor and he coolly informed me, 'Yes, in most people, the chemo does stop your periods.'

'Will they come back when the chemo is over?'

He patiently answered, 'Sometimes they do, and sometimes they don't. There is no fixed time period. You are forty-five. They might not come back, and you might have forced menopause.'

Menopause! Now I also have menopause to deal with. Just like that, with no warning.

First, it was hard to not have my period. I've always had a great relationship with my period. Comes on time, no pain, normal flow, just some back ache at the most. I've trekked in the monsoon on my period. That's how easy it's been for me. And as a result, I've always regarded my period to be a great indicator that everything in my body is working fine.

Having my period just stop came as a shock to me. First, I had no time to adjust to it. One day it was gone. Second, it told me that however much I stay positive, do yoga, eat well, play BFF-BFF with chemo, I had to face the facts. My body was not okay. I was trying to do everything for it. But that's how it was going to be. The chemo would have side effects that I did not want to accept.

And menopause? Ooh boy. So much unbidden stuff rushed into my head. Menopause means I'm now old. Off the shelf. In a dusty, dowdy little corner. How could that be? I was fit and slim and beautiful a couple of months back. And now you tell me I'm over the hill, and past my prime.

And I didn't know what to expect. Would I have mood swings, would I put on weight, would I grow hair on my stomach? Bloody hell, why is menopause so hushed up? Why has no one prepared me for this?

What also came as a shock to me was the hot flashes. What the hell is that!

Let me describe it to you. I'm sitting there talking to someone, like all normal. And the next second, my face is on fire and I'm sweating like a pig. That person is wondering what effect they are having on me!

Or I'm sleeping, it's great weather, the fan is on full speed. And suddenly I wake up, feeling like I'm in the Sahara Desert. It is so hot. And I'm sweating again.

It's not just uncomfortable, it's also very disconcerting. A hot flash can happen any time. And you keep wondering what people are thinking, watching you suddenly start to sweat like a steam engine.

I'm mourning the loss of my period, I have no hair, I'm sweating at the drop of a hat, I am jealous of my friends, I have menopause, I am superstitious. Fuck. Who the hell am I?!

26

ᘯ

Somewhere in the latter half of my chemo protocol, there was a shift. I still found it hard to come to terms with everything that was happening to me, but I realized I had to stop controlling things, and take each day as it came.

The four big chemos? They had progressively gotten harder on my body. I felt tired faster, foggier, and even though I tried to keep myself going physically, by the fourth chemo I was wiped out.

The twelve smaller chemos, they were so much easier. Because they were weekly, they weren't as potent, and my body was doing better, I was feeling sharper. But my sharper mind was now giving me hell.

It was playing games with me. I was terrified of getting a relapse, I was scared that the chemo might not do its job. I was scared of dying, I was scared of spending my life like this. I'd feel lonely. I'd feel crowded. I'd feel loved. I'd feel ugly.

And around my twelfth chemo, I just crashed. I had the worst attack of the blues. It was so bad that even I got scared. It was like one half of me couldn't stop crying hysterically, and one half of me was watching that half and going, 'Dude, I'm worried for her.'

I had to speak to someone. Not someone who loved me, but someone who had been through this. I messaged Himanshu. In my

199

heart, I had no hope. I thought he'd just try and cheer me up, and or tell me I got this.

Instead, he heard me out, and then reminded me of a trek we had gone on.

About two years before all this happened, Himanshu, another friend, and I made an impromptu plan to head for a trek to Uttarakhand. Being foolhardy Mumbaikars, we never accounted for the fact that a trek in August would mean you are going to be trekking inside your own personal waterfall.

Pumped up about everything, including long visits to Decathlon, which in our heads prepared us for everything (we couldn't have been more wrong), we set off.

The first day of the trek we walked for about six hours to reach our destination. It was all uphill, and our city legs were getting used to walking and scrambling. We passed fields and villages, and it was breathtaking.

From there each day got harder. It just kept pouring as we climbed. We struggled with our breath as the rain snaked in through our ponchos. Our shoes kept sinking into the mud. And suddenly, those same apple orchards no longer looked breathtaking.

The most challenging was the fourth day. We were headed for a peak called Vijay Top. Upwards of 12,500 feet. We started early that morning, knowing it was going to be a long and exhausting day. It was cloudy and misty. I remember lacing up my shoes that were still soaked from crossing streams the day before. My shorts were caked with slush. My waterproof poncho was smelling worse than the mules carrying our food. But I was beyond caring.

So, we started our climb. Now the thing about treks is they are very lonely. However big or small a group you are in, this is your trek, your struggle, your heart, your breath. And finally, your thoughts. I had decided to keep myself very small when the trek got hard. Which means I would practise shrinking into myself. Just go into my body like a turtle. Till all that exists is my heart and my breathing. I cease to be there. My hands and feet can be cold and soggy, but I don't feel it. I only see trees, smell the mountain air, and shut myself from the rain. But more than that, for large parts, I just look down at the path and keep walking.

It started raining heavily just as we set off. And then came the landslides. Huge parts of the mountains had caved in. Which means we had to go down new paths, which weren't really paths. They were slippery and tricky, and we had to clamber around uprooted trees, boulders, and keep moving. Because after four days, heading back was not an option. It would be just as painful.

Now, the thing with landslides is, you have to sometimes go all the way down before you can come up. True of all treks, but particularly true that day. So, we'd touch the bottom, right down at the end of the valley, where there would be silent streams, dark and moist trees dripping water on your head when you sat under them to catch your breath, and hardly any light or rain filtering in. And then we'd start the long and treacherous climb uphill again. We did this at least thrice that day.

Finally, we reached a place where it was all uphill. And in your head, you start thinking this could be the way to the top. But it isn't. Because the top is still very far.

So, you go back to staring at the path, letting your mind drain out till there's no thought but just a voice telling you to surrender to this pain and discomfort. Your body takes over. One foot in front of the other. Your head is bent, so the rain doesn't run in front of your eyes. And you keep breathing, and you keep going.

You know the top will come. And you will have chai and Maggi, and the exhaustion will give way to exhilaration.

But you know this is the time to keep pushing on.

You also know that after eight hours of this, you will have changed. You will know you are capable of being strong, you will trust your body like crazy, you will learn that you can switch off the voices in your head.

You will also know that to reach Vijay Top, it takes many dark, gloomy forest floors that you will have to descend into.

I'm grateful for that day. The lessons it taught me rescued me the day when I felt there was no hope.

I knew that from here onwards, the only thing I could do was put one foot in front of the other.

27

Before you think I was only a nauseous, fissure-assed philosopher through my treatment, I wasn't.

Those nine months taught me a lot of stuff.

First, it taught me that most people are well-meaning, but also batshit crazy. The minute I started talking about my diagnosis and what was happening to me, there was an outpouring of love and concern. And in that deluge of emotion, people sent me article links with messages like, 'Shorms, I read this and I thought about you.'

Excellent. Because the article is about someone, somewhere in the world who got cancer and died. Died. Finished. Khallas. Lights off. Now which part of that article reminded you of me?

If it wasn't that, then it would be a link with a message, 'Shorms, you are my hero. Please read this.'

Read it? The lady in the article had a relapse. Thrice. And you think I'm going to enjoy reading this. Why?

I'm convinced most people didn't even read what they were sending me, they just saw the word 'cancer' in the headline and passed it on.

Second, it taught me how much I was loved. By my parents, who put their lives on hold so they could be there for me. They'd literally fly down before every chemo, wait till I felt better and then go back, and then do this all over again. They lived out of suitcases for that entire period. Only so I could be looked after, and yet have my space. As my chemo progressed, they also learned to deal with it. There were days when we'd laugh, they'd take me for long drives in the rain, they'd cook my favourite food. It was always going to be hard watching their daughter go through this. But soon they realized I was not faking it to be strong, that I genuinely was okay. I was healing and the biggest breakthrough was when one morning, instead of saying the usual 'your illness', my mother actually said the words, 'cancer'. I stopped feeling guilty, they stopped feeling destroyed, and we realized that through it all, we could still smile.

Those nine months also released me. I spent more time with Anirban. It was like a blank slate; we were starting all over again. He saw me at my most vulnerable. And I saw him as the person who, instinctively, I trusted and needed the most. Only he could change my dressing, only he could bathe me, only he could hold me every single time I thought I couldn't do it. And he did it with such grace and ease. He never gave me platitudes, he never questioned my madcap ways. And the days I cried, he just held me, and I felt his tears on my face. I think we were crying that this is what it took for us to realize that we were meant to be together.

Let me digress, and tell you, it's not easy being married. And we got married when we were kids. Twenty-two and twenty-three. But let me also tell you, that sometimes it takes cancer to tell you that this is the person you want to grow old with. This is the only person who truly gets you.

In my head, I always pictured it as two swimmers in the open sea. Slowly drifting apart. First, it's okay. Then it gets scary. The distance is widening, and you don't know how to close it. And then there's a cyclone, and the winds howl and you are tossed around, battered and bruised, but guess what, you can suddenly see the other person. And there's no one else you want to see. And you hold on to each other.

Scared out of your wits, but also deliriously happy to have found each other again.

Then there were my friends. Oinx, who cancelled her holiday abroad. Ziba, who can never wake up early, came for every early morning appointment. My friends and partners at work, Parag and Dixit, who for nine months did their share of work, and mine too. It was bloody hard for them, especially since one day I was at work and in their lives, and the next day I was gone. But they never once said anything to me except, 'All you have to do is beat this.'

Also, it's not just the things people say to you that tells you they love you. It's the things they do. My friends and family tolerated everything. One day I decided to call an acupuncturist. No one rolled their eyes at me. The man arrived, didn't listen to a word of what I said, pressed some points in my hand, and gave me a headache.

Another time I decided, in the middle of my chemo, to learn rifle shooting. Again, my friends and family gamely agreed to it. In fact, two of my friends even signed up for it, and went to classes with me. I wanted to paint, friends and strangers came and painted with me. I was cranky, and wanted to see people. My colleagues came and played games with me. My in-laws, Koeli didi, friends, colleagues, strangers on Instagram and Twitter, ex-colleagues, friends I hadn't met in years. They made time, they showed up, with food, paints, books, games.

It's incredible how everyone enveloped me with love.

The third thing was my realization that as my physical struggle with the chemo reduced, my fight with my mind became more serious. And I think in the end that's what made me stronger. I was never in a fight with my body, it was always my mind that I had to control.

After my first four big chemos were over, my chemo protocol moved to weekly chemos. And I remember, I got back home from the first weekly chemo, and I felt human. The joy! I wasn't foggy or feeling like this person who was stuffed with chemicals and had to spend a week trying to find her way out of it. I could eat, and sleep, and the next day my system wasn't rebelling. It was much easier.

Also, the weekly chemo did not include the horrid Red Devil Rooh Afza.

We soon fell into a rhythm over those twelve weeks. Anirban and I could look beyond the initial months of struggle and coping, and now just follow a pattern on autopilot. The blood tests every week before my chemo, going to the hospital, organizing my things, getting my food pass, reaching the hospital early, it was Groundhog Day. Everything in a loop. And I was superstitious. I would take the same food, the clothes, the same water bottle, and the same Mother Mary statue.

The chemo doctor had also said that this particular medicine they were giving during my weekly chemo could cause joint pains. But he was also very kick-ass, as he looked straight at me and told me that he could prescribe medicines, but there was already a lot going into my body. So instead, his advice to me would be to walk three to five kilometres a day.

I don't know if this was a theory that he made up, or if walking actually helps. But in my case, I just walked my way through the chemo. It's the thing that propelled me, that gave me some sense of purpose. I think I took one foot in front of the other literally. Some days I'd struggle, and I'd give up after three kilometres, but most days I'd manage five. I'd take pictures, explore by-lanes, look at old bungalows, it was liberating in a way. I'd never been home during the day, and suddenly there I was, at all these odd times, walking the streets of my neighbourhood. I looked odd, but my head was clearing. Much later, Ziba told me that I looked like a sight, bald head, moon face, sneakers, tights, T-shirt, raincoat tied around my waist (the Mumbai monsoons had arrived by then), and an umbrella in my hand. Striding through Bandra.

And once I found my feet, I learnt to silence my mind. All the fear and insecurities, they didn't leave me, but I outpaced them most days. I decided to learn rifle shooting. The people at the shooting gallery were at first a bit shook, and then really nice to me once they realized I was being treated for cancer. Then I started learning pottery. It was therapy. Sometimes, I'd want to beat the clay into shape, and sometimes I was happy sinking my hands into it.

It didn't mean that I didn't have bad days. There were lots of them. The last stretch was hard. I have a name for it. It's the sushi syndrome. Instead of focusing on how amazing the sushi tastes, half the time I'm worried about one plate of sushi or two. One plate is never enough and two is way too much. I'm never able to enjoy it properly, because my mind is only focusing on why I can't just get one and a half plates!

And now, the sushi syndrome wasn't letting me enjoy the fact that it was going to end. Instead, I was only wondering, what if I had a relapse? How could anyone be sure that the chemo was working? Why were they not going to do another PET scan? What happens after this? How am I going to stay safe?

The great part is, every time my mind ran around in circles, the universe sent me a gift. Like Ameeta. Who I met on Instagram. Who was also being treated for breast cancer at the same time.

Now here is the story. We have someone in common who follows us both on Instagram. This person writes to Ameeta about me. And Ameeta replies, but accidentally sends it to my inbox.

Actually, there are no accidents. It was meant to be that we'll bump into each other somehow. We discovered we were both being treated for the same form of breast cancer, in the same city, but in different hospitals. And we were both going through our weekly chemo. She was ahead of me by two chemos, but apart from that everything was the same. Including the fact that both of us had chemo on Monday morning.

We started a Monday morning ritual. Checking in with each other.

All the best.

Has your chemo started?

My medicines haven't arrived as yet.

I'm almost done.

Leaving for home. You have a good week.

It was a mirror, to have someone going through it, exactly the same protocol, at the same time. We were strangers, but we immediately had this bond. What we felt and we told each other, no one would get as instinctively as we did. Fun fact is we've never met, not even when it got over.

Then there was a girl who reached out to me on Instagram. She had just been diagnosed and her surgery was coming up. She wanted to know what it would be like, particularly the reconstruction. She was going to lose her nipple as well, and had no idea how the nipple area would look with the grafting. We had been talking on video calls, and I trusted her, so I finally asked, 'Do you want to see what it looks like?' And she said yes, if I didn't mind.

I took a picture of my reconstructed boob and I sent it to her. And in my head, I'm laughing. I'm sending a boob picture, on Instagram, to a stranger! Only this is not the way I'd have ever seen that play out.

Also, my relationship with 'new boob' was improving. There were days when I was sad, because I was now a one nipple freak. But on most days, I was just happy that it was going to be over, and I had a lovely new boob to stuff into a bra. And I had cleavage. Hallelujah!

I don't know how the universe had such great stalking skills, but it just knew when I needed help.

There was one day when I was really low. I think this was towards the end, when I had that bad attack of the blues. Ganesh, my yoga teacher, came home, and I set up my mat, sat down, and much to my own horror, burst into tears. Ganesh didn't look fazed. I kept telling him between sobs that I was very low and I was so scared. Now that the end was near, it was like I was having problems accepting that my treatment was going to be over, and I had done it.

Ganesh produced a set of cards from his bag. And very gently told me that I would get my answer in these cards. I couldn't pick more than three, because the answer would come within three cards. I looked at him, he looked very serious, and so I picked a card. I turned it around and it said something like you are beautiful.

Whatever. Bullshit.

I picked another card. And again, it said something generic, that didn't do anything for me.

Then I picked the third and final card. And all it said was: Trust the universe.

Ta-da. That was it. It was about trusting. All the love, all the chemo, all the trees in my lane, the birds I saw from my window, the sky, the breeze, the sea. I just had to surrender to the universe.

And something clicked. Suddenly, I couldn't wait to celebrate the end of my chemo.

Which brings me to that day. Now the thing is, for months this has been my goalpost. This is what I've wanted more than anything. And it suddenly feels like it can't be a normal day. I want Karan Johar to meet Sanjay Leela Bhansali and plan a production for my last chemo. I want music on the street, rose petals to be flung from every window of Kokilaben Hospital, drums being played, synchronized dancers at every corner.

I buy a cake for the nurses, with icing that says 'thank you' in Malayalam. Gifts for my doctors. I plan my clothes. I wear lipstick. And I just can't stop grinning. When I walk out of chemo ward on that day, I want everybody on the floor to stop and sing out, 'You made it.'

So Anirban makes up for it by hugging me like crazy and taking videos of me walking out of the ward.

Now I have twenty consecutive sessions of radiation to go. And I'm not scared. Dude, I just finished sixteen chemos. Till I start hearing the radiation horror stories. Apparently, there are people who were okay through their chemo, and then went all pukey sick during their radiation. Some people told me about radiation burns and scars. And how your throat starts to close.

So once again, it was time to bring out my big girl underwear and go into turtle mode.

First thing that happened was I moved my radiation to a hospital close to home. It was awesome, a middle-class version of Kokilaben Hospital, where they didn't care about food passes and you could bring a whole vegetable cart with you for tiffin.

My radiologist was a man with piercing eyes, and a big tika on his head. He ran a tight ship. And I just trusted him from day one.

The only thing that scared me was when he said that the radiation could affect my heart, because it was my left breast. I had to do breathing exercises a week before radiation, where I'd puff my chest and hold my breath, so they get that gap between my chest and my heart while delivering the radiation.

The radiation would be over in ten minutes at the most. Of course, this meant lying on my back and staring at the ceiling, with one breast exposed, while everyone went about their work. I think there's a very small population of people in Mumbai who have not seen my reconstructed boob!

Another thing that changed was, I went for radiation by myself. I immediately felt better. I was independent, after months and months of being dependent on everyone. I think it was that high that saw me through the radiation.

Apart from a mild discomfort in my throat, I got through the radiation just counting down to the days when it would be over. I remember this one incident. The waiting room at the radiation place was small. And there was another lady, who was coming for radiation every day, around the same time as me. By then, I was so superstitious that I would usually avoid eye contact with anyone, because the first thing people would ask was 'Side effects?' I was convinced that if I told anyone that this was relatively easy for me, I'd jinx it, so I would diligently look down at my Kindle.

Except for this lady, who would not take averted eyes as a no. She would literally poke me and dig her elbow into me, and ask me, 'Side effects?' And I'd just mumble, till she finally got frustrated, and rattled off a long list of complaints and side effects to me. This went on every day. I couldn't take it any longer. And one day I decided, I'll just make up a long list of side effects and get her off my back. So that day, when she dug her elbow into me, I started. For ten minutes I just recited every problem I could think of. She kept looking at me till I finished. I was exhausted, but pleased that she would be happy. Instead, she fixed me with a cold look and said, 'We must be grateful for what we have. And not complain and count our side effects.'

The radiation didn't burn me, she did!

And then, it was the day of my last radiation. Nine long months of treatment coming to an end. Everyone was so excited, Anirban, my parents, friends, family. I was all cool and chill, and I told everyone that nobody needs to come with me, because I got this. Ziba however, insisted on coming with me. I kept telling her she doesn't need to, but she wouldn't take no for an answer.

She's in the waiting room, I finish my radiation, say thank you to all the nurses and the technicians, walk out, take one look at Ziba, and start bawling my eyes out. It was done, I could cry as much as I wanted now!

And here's the best part. The universe, in keeping with being so kind to me, sent me a sign that morning. When Ziba and I left my building for my radiation, as we turned the corner, I looked out of the car window, and right across the street from me, the sun shining on him, stood Shahid Kapoor. Without his shirt!

I kid you not.

He was shooting for the film *Kabir Singh* and standing right there without his shirt.

It's like the universe said, 'Shormistha, you've gone through a shit year, and it's over now. Here's a gift for you. Shirtless Shahid!'

The End.

A Postscript on Life After

First, when you're bald and crying, and people tell you after chemo your hair will grow back thicker, you don't believe them. At least I didn't. But I was wrong. I now have thick, long hair.

It's another matter that thanks to the oestrogen suppressants I have thick, long hair on my face and arms too.

But it's okay. I have discovered that Kanchan, the lady who saved my hoo-ha from the newbie nurse and her razor, can also wax my face off.

Second, in the long run, having one less nipple is fine. And so is having a reconstructed boob. Though I still don't know how anyone would opt for it willingly. Not because I'm judging, but because it has no feeling. You know you are squishing something, but it might as well be a stress ball in your hand. Still, it makes me feel good because it fills out a dress.

Third, you're chill. Dude, I went through cancer. That's the first thought in my head when things are not going okay. And suddenly everything seems relatively unimportant. For instance, I'm still a little scared of flying sometimes, but then I just think, I went through sixteen chemos! And it's sorted.

I say no more often. I'm nicer to myself. I take time out to travel. I love being around Anirban. I talk to my parents about things that

213

matter. I'm not the obsessed-with-work, anti-social person I was. I actively pursue my hobbies.

And guess what, menopause is just fine. Sweaty suits me, adds a sheen to my face. For too long, this shit has been kept under wraps. I'm not past my prime or off the shelf or a 'poor thing'. I'm just getting older, and that's fine. I can still do everything I want, without some eggs getting in the way.

Wait a minute. It took cancer to sort a midlife crisis! Damn, next time, universe, just deal me a sports car or something.

Acknowledgements

This has to start with the men and women who changed my life. My doctor's. Each one of them is so passionate about what they do. It just blows my mind how much they care, and how hard they work. Dr Shilpa Lad who was so kind when she diagnosed me. And continues to be a part of my life, with her mission to break taboos around breast cancer. Dr Mandar Nadkarni, who is a star, not just because he's the best surgeon in the world and saved my life, but also because he has so much empathy and is just too cool for school. Dr Quazi Ahmad, who gave me a whole new breast and cleavage (hurrah!) and smiled at my attempts at getting him to take fat off my hips. Dr Imran, who gave me the gift of walking, and saw me through my chemos with a smile. What's incredible is each of these doctors said yes to me using their real names, because they were so happy I was writing a book that spoke about my experience.

Most of us will never know how committed doctors are, and how much they believe in what they do. But I'm grateful to have had an opportunity to realize that.

Also, a big thanks to all the other doctors I came across, nurses and staff at Kokilaben Hospital. Especially the nurses at the chemo ward, who grin and stay calm through everything. You are the best chechi's I could have ever asked for.

215

The doctors at Tata Memorial who were my first port of call. Hats off to you guys. Just looking at the sheer number of people who land up at your door makes me realize that everyone who works there, or worked there, is made of something else. You all have my respect. Also, the wonderful radiation department at Hinduja Hospital, Mahim under Dr V. Kannan. I think my radiation experience was so smooth only because every single person in that department was so pleasant and super-efficient. Dr Nitesh Rohatgi, you might not remember me, but your advice on making it easier for myself and not feeling guilty, freed me and helped so much. And finally, my GP, whose name I've changed, but who is the most wonderful GP. Dr Sewanti Limaye, thank you for giving me great advice and making me feel good every time I saw you.

Manisha, we've never met. But you were my first setting, and you set the course for everything. Lawrence, thank you for being an insurance agent who was on my side, from day one.

Next is my super editor, Sonal Nerurkar at HarperCollins. Who started talking to me in 2018. And patiently waited for my treatment to end, then another year for me to stop celebrating before she cracked the whip! She's given me the best feedback, steadied me through phases of 'I don't want to do this', and been the best editor a debut author could ask for. My agent Jayapriya Vasudevan at Jacaranda Books, who works quietly and firmly, just what the doctor prescribed for me. Amit Malhotra and Diya Kar at HarperCollins, a big thank you to you as well.

My friends, who came for chemos, waited with my parents during my surgery, fed me, sent me gifts, played games with me, painted with me, walked with me, travelled across cities and even Mira Road! Ziba and Oinx, for the insane amount of love and madness. I felt like I was enveloped in a warm blanket, the whole time. Tarini, for wheatgrass, chemo ward visits, Agatha Christie hard disks. Gauri, for the paints, the worry, the love. Vidhya, for coming to the hospital and for loving me. Parag, for the million walks, the worry, the messages, the company. Himanshu, for being my guide. Nupur, for also being my guide, and helping me navigate my way through good and bad days. Andy, for the daily calls.

Kartik, Dixit, Amit, Kavita, Ruchi, Sanju, Ritz, Kalyan, Kainaz, Ipsita, Amrita, Anand, Abhishek, thank you for spending time with me, feeding me, cheering me on. Oh, and the number of gifts I got. If I count all my gifts over various birthdays (and at 48 that's a lot of birthdays) even then I wouldn't have got so many. Thank you everyone who sent me stuff, from books, to Archie Digests to paints to hampers of healthy food. Sajid Wajid Shaikh, for being a stranger who never felt like a stranger.

Atul and Rupa, my flower remedy doctors. Who were so certain I'll be fine. Tulip, my nutritionist and friend, for constantly checking on me. And all my yoga teachers, with a special shout out to Diipti, and my forever favourite Ganesh. Who made me realize I was way stronger than I gave myself credit for.

Everyone at Flying Cursor. Actually, everyone who ever worked at Flying Cursor. You guys really made me feel very loved. With prayers, messages, pep talks, mails, videos. It was nine months of missing y'all and yet feeling that all of you are right there for me. Diana, Amin, Delon, your prayers meant a lot. Nivedita and Divya, how can I ever forget those emails. Tejas, Bipin and Ajay, special shout out to you guys. Everyone at Rickshaw, I might not work there anymore, but I still feel the love. And of course, so many of my clients. Who reached out to me, and supported Flying Cursor, and my partners Parag, Dixit and Tejas.

Shiny, for the cycling, the calm when the storm broke, and of course being such a big part of this book. The cover design, the illustrations, the laughter, the long chats, I'm worried sometimes that you've started reading my mind.

My chemo ward friends, friends who read my blogs, Nandita, Roohi, friends of my parents' friends who read my blogs. It all added up. Jugal, who pointed me towards the ladies at The Ladies Finger, Durga and Nandagopal, you all helped my voice travel. It was a big deal to be able to tell people what I was going through, so thank you.

My cancer survivor friends Rupal and Sanjukta. Ameeta, whom I have never met, but we will forever be bound together, in health and happiness. Anant, for the songs, the calls and the advice. Mahesh and Sharda, for the post treatment mending. Sapna, Kiran, Mad O Wot, for all the buzz cuts. Kanchan, for the waxing that saved my life!

Aditi Mittal, you are the kindest, most generous person ever. Anuja Chauhan, damn, I've always looked up to you. Nisha Susan, thank you for your kind words. The Ladies Finger is where it all started. You guys really made my day, by reading the manuscript. Swati Bhattacharya, another person I look up to. Thank you for always being so warm and encouraging.

All my Instagram friends. There are just so many people who pinged me, bolstered me, and loved me so fiercely. I am grateful to all of you. Vinita and Vineeta, thank you for being my Insta cheerleaders. My 30 Bondel Road gang. Shoma ma'am, Shilpa ma'am, and and my sister in kathak, Sheetal. Nriyanidhi and you all gave me so much love.

Vijaya, Laxmi Tai, Lata. For looking after me, and my house.

All my aunts, uncles, cousins. The family groups were buzzing, Facebook comments were full of we love you, and you look beautiful. I am so grateful for the love.

Koeli didi. I don't know how many trips you made. Thank you for being the most awesome company, who did yoga, watched movies, meditated, painted, did every single crackpot thing I wanted to do, with so much enthusiasm. I love you so much. Ma and Baba. For being there, being worried, but trying hard not to show it, and instead showing it through all the food that was cooked for me. Love you lots. Anushka and Anand, this goes for you mad folks as well.

Milo and Tuggu, my zoo. For curling up next to me, putting their head on my lap and comforting me every time I cried. Milo, I will miss you forever.

Mom and Dad. I kept this for the end, because I knew I'd be blinking back tears. We went through a storm, and we came out stronger. Thank you for everything you have done for me. And more than that, thank you for a wonderful childhood and the gift of independence that you gave me. You are my heart. I can't not mention the Indian Air Force in the acknowledgments. Such a large part of my happiest memories. And the military hospitals. My childhood memories may be of measles and mumps, but gratitude to all doctors, nurses and staff who work there, and have looked after Mom, Dad and even me from time to time. Once an Air Force kid, always an Air Force kid.

Anirban. Dude, I just lucked out when I met you. You are my family, my safe place, my happy holiday.

And finally, Shaoli. There's not a day I don't miss you. You would have been so happy to see this book. My guide to how to live my life, you'll always remain a part of my heart. And Amit da. My god, you would have made such a big deal about this book. I still find it hard to accept that both of you are not a part of my life anymore. But I hope you've met each other and are chilling somewhere, because this book is a toast to both of you, for showing us that you can live life with such happiness and joy.

About the Author

Shormistha Mukherjee mixes travel with history, saris with sneakers, feni with Limca. Co-founder of a digital agency, she ran a very popular blog as agentgreenglass and has written a short fiction series for Juggernaut. She's most grateful to have survived breast cancer and for being given another chance to make the most of her life.